LITERARY CRITICISM OF R.S. CRANE

THEORY AND PRACTICE

ASIT KR. BISWAS

ATLANTIC
PUBLISHERS & DISTRIBUTORS

Published by
ATLANTIC PUBLISHERS AND DISTRIBUTORS
B-2, Vishal Enclave, Opp. Rajouri Garden, New Delhi-110027
Phones : 25413460, 25429987, 25466842

Sales Office
7/22, Ansari Road, Darya Ganj, New Delhi-110002
Phones : 23273880, 23285873, 23280451
Fax : 91-11-23285873
web : www.atlanticbooks.com
e-mail : info@atlanticbooks.com

ISBN 81-269-0276-0

Typeset at
APD Computer Graphics, Delhi
Printed in India at
Nice Printing Press, Delhi

To Professor Mohit K. Ray

—My Philosopher and Guide.

FOREWORD

I am glad to write this foreword to *Literary Criticism of R.S. Crane: Theory and Practice* of Dr. Asit Kumar Biswas. The book is a revised and updated version of his doctoral dissertation on Crane which he had done under my supervision about a decade ago. I have immensely enjoyed reading it.

R.S. Crane (1886-1967) did not receive the recognition which he so eminently deserved. Recognition of Crane's value as a critic has been slow in coming mainly because of the intemperate essays he wrote in the beginning of his critical career as an angry young critic. In these essays he suggested that the critical languages of Empson, Richards, Cleanth Brooks and R.B. Heilman, among others, are not worth considering, for he found Richards 'guilty of psychologism,' Brooks 'too limited in his concept of poetry as irony,' Heilman 'reducing *King Lear* to a cluster of patterned imageries,' and Empson a 'juggler of ambiguity.' To Crane, the most important exponent of the Chicago Aristotelians, Aristotle is the only theorist who devised a rational scheme to study poems as a class of objects, as concrete artistic wholes. According to Crane, all subsequent criticism considered poems only as modes of discourse as a result of which criticism became increasingly concerned with the general poetic qualities rather than with the concrete works. This approach led to proliferation of critical theories so much so that in the crossfire of critical theories literature itself was about to become a casualty. Rejecting, therefore, all the versions of dogmatism and scepticism Crane propounds the theory of critical pluralism. His point is that the subject matter of criticism is the literary work itself but the reality that criticism investigates is too complex to be subsumed in any one particular theory.

In his illuminating book Dr. Biswas has very clearly shown that as a critical theorist Crane is a pluralist and in practice he keeps on exploring the possibility of extending the principle and methods of Aristotle's *poetics*. Assiduously mapping out Crane's critical theory in all his major writings and by making a fine critical analysis of Crane's practical criticism Dr. Biswas has brought under sharp focus the value of critical pluralism as enunciated and practised by Crane, and has established convincingly that no other approach can do comparable justice to the diversity of literary works and multidimensional perspectivity of a literary work. The best way, and possibly the only way, to reconcile the literary autonomy and the literary relevance, or the literal and the 'dialectical' is the pluralistic approach. By restoring Crane to his rightful position in the history of modern criticism Dr. Biswas has done a great service to Crane. Justice is done at last to Ronald Salmon Crane.

Dr. Biswas is a shy and soft-spoken person like Chaucer's 'Clerk of Oxenford,' but as the reader begins to plod through his book he will realize how lightly he carries his scholarship that is evident in the fine insightful flashes that make this luminous study of the criticism of R.S. Crane such an enjoyable and intellectually stimulating reading. Criticism is not everybody's cup of tea. It is avoided by most research scholars as something very dry and difficult. And to write on Crane—one of the most difficult and controversial, and, therefore, neglected critics—is not an easy job. But Dr. Biswas has done this difficult task he set upon himself extremely well.

I am sure all the students of literary criticism will find this book quite useful and interesting.

MOHIT K. RAY

PREFACE

Literary criticism has received enormous attention since the beginning of the last century and has gradually developed almost as an independent discipline by virtue of its own merit. Following the huge knowledge explosion in the various fields of human activities and its growing impacts on contemporary literature, various critical theories have been developed. Literary criticism, one must admit, is a reasoned discourse on literature. And literary theories are some effective tools which may successfully be used for a fruitful judgment of the literary texts. But when some new knowledge is reflected in some literary texts, the old critical tools are of less or of no use to judge the new literary elements. Hence, new theories are formed. This is one important way how in the twentieth century a overwhelming variety of critical theories like Marxist criticism, New criticism, Psychoanalytical criticism, Archetypal criticism, Reader-response criticism, Feministic criticism, Structuralism, and presently Deconstructionism have emerged. These theories, one must admit, have also made the twentieth century critical scenario an enriched but at the same time a very complicated one. Significantly, each of the theories has its validity in its own way and contributes to the understanding and analysis of a literary text. But the problem arises when each group of critical theorists claims its superiority over others in solving various critical problems. A young scholar or a university student is often puzzled to find that different groups of critics prescribe different approaches or theoretical ends with regard to the same set of critical questions.

It is in this area of confusion or bewilderment in the complicated world of critical *isms* of the 20th century that R.S. Crane's critical observations and theoretical precepts throw some very useful light. The leader of the Chicago school of criticism, Crane (1886-1967) shows us the way toward a multiple response to a literary text, which is always multidimensional. Crane also shows how various critical theories may be of immense help, if properly employed, for better understanding of literary texts of diversified natures. He has emphasised the need for a pluralistic view of literature, offering at the same time a workable method for that purpose. Crane has also pointed out the lacunae of the New Criticism—and that was done at a time when the New Criticism was in its full flourish and was enjoying the greatest currency in the field of literary criticism. All these make Crane quite valid and worth studying even in the present century. A humble effort has been made in this book to evaluate the critical position of R.S. Crane and to show how the readers may benefit from his critical insights in our understanding and evaluation of different literary texts. I will consider my labour fruitful if my book is found to help young critics and scholars in clarifying as well as broadening their critical understanding and analytic mind.

However, I must take advantage of the occasion to express my sincerest regard and gratitude to those without whose help and inspiration the publication of this book would have been impossible. Among these well-wishers the first and the foremost is my respected teacher Dr. Mohit K. Ray, Professor of English of the University of Burdwan (West Bengal). It is he who has developed in me, by means of his scholarly discussions and constant encouragement, the mind for critical and scholarly pursuits. I am always in his debt. I must also convey my sincere gratitude to my colleagues in the Department of English as well as in some other departments of Bankura Christian College who have encouraged me to publish the book. The Principal of the college, Dr. Richard R.N. Bajpai, who is never tired of encouraging me in my scholarly pursuits has also made me profoundly thankful to him. Finally, Dr. K.R. Gupta, Managing Director of M/s Atlantic Publishers and Distributors, New Delhi, has made me indebted to him by publishing the book with utmost care. No amount of thanks is enough for him.

ASIT KR. BISWAS

CONTENTS

1

TWENTIETH CENTURY CRITICAL SCENARIO: FROM THE BEGINNING TO *THE NEW CRITICISM* (1941)

If the advent of modernism is something more than a mere historical event it must be admitted that literary criticism in the United States achieved modernity not before the second decade of the twentieth century. I say this, firstly, because of the fact, as Glicksberg has pointed out, that "before 1910 there was little criticism of American literature" (Glicksberg 9). America was still engaged, in the early years of the 20th century, in the preceding century's search for a sense of national identity. The country lacked remarkably the creative confidence and courage to establish a respectable ideal especially in the field of literary criticism. And secondly, because the early 20th century America followed, to a great extent, the romantic and Victorian ideas and ideals so far as literary art and criticism were concerned. In those years, Rene Wellek observes, "the United States was still ruled by what, in 1911, Santayana labelled the 'Genteel Tradition,' a variant of Victorianism, of vapid, derivative idealism" (Wellek 1). The first remarkable voice against this vapid idealism was, of course, that of H.L. Mencken, whose relatively small amount of writing on literary criticism had a great impact on the ensuing change of a general taste and outlook during and after the first world war.

However, literary criticism in America had its rapid development from the second decade of the 20th century, and within a very short time it achieved a remarkable place beside the contemporary European criticism and culture. Before the most remarkable critical movement of the century, I mean the New Criticism, there were in the field of American literary criticism at least three major trends under the names of Impressionism, New Humanism and Marxist Criticism, each one of which has left a distinguished mark in the history of literary criticism.

My intention, however, is not to give a historical account of the various critical movements. Nor do I intend to find out the respective values of these movements. My intention is rather to study the reason why so many critical theories come to exist as well as to point out the fault which is common to all of them. It will help us immensely to realise the critical scenario in which the Chicago school of critics led by R.S. Crane, emerged in the middle of the century.

It should be borne in mind that the birth of a new theory or idea in literary criticism is never whimsical or out of the track. Generally, the limitations of the past ideas on the one hand and the literary position—the demand of the literary works of a certain period—on the other are two of the major stimuli behind the birth of a new critical theory, whatever it may be. Not only that, a new theory may also be the function of some new knowledge, which modifies our experience of life and literature. As our knowledge about life and society broadens, the existing outlooks and attitudes undergo magnificent changes. It is then that a new theory often emerges to meet the needs of the changed situations, caused by the new revelations in the field of knowledge. Psychoanalytical criticism, for example, developed into a system when the psychoanalytical theories of Freud and Jung made the critics aware of the role of the subconscious in any creative endeavour. The literary artists also consciously exploited their newly acquired knowledge of psychology in their works. The subconscious is thus artistically exploited in literary works as a result of which the existing critical theories became, to some extent at least, inadequate for proper evaluation of this new element, and this inadequacy of the previous theories led to the growth of psychoanalytical criticism.

These are, therefore, some of the points which explain the reasons of the existence of different critical theories in the realm of literary criticism. They also make it clear that we can hardly deny the necessity of a new method to judge and evaluate the newer elements in literature better. In fact, each and every critical theory highlights or takes into its special consideration some aspect which were either overlooked, or neglected, or not anticipated in the past theories. Each theory has thus its specific value.

But the problem arises when any particular critical school claims to have the only and possibly the best method, in suppersession of all the previous ones considered as incomplete and inadequate. They fall a victim to their monistic approaches and dogmatic stands. No critical theory before that of the Chicago school of critics—Impressionism, New Humanism, Marxist Criticism or the New Criticism—is free from this fault. Each of them neglects certain aspects in its over-enthusiasm of giving special attention to and emphasis on some others, and at the same time tries to establish itself as the only valid method of criticism. They fail to realize what Harry Levin said in 1957. "Literature," he said, "appeals to so many values, aesthetic and otherwise, that it requires a pluralistic approach" (Levin 257).

The New Humanists of the 20th century, for example, like most of the 19th century European and American critics were so much preoccupied with the extra-textual factors like the question of morality that they could pay only a little attention to the aesthetic elements in a literary work. An extreme preoccupation with the ethical elements in literature restricted their critical evaluation; and in consequence they failed to create a positive line of criticism. Paul Elmer More, for example, fostered the view that before evaluating a piece of literary work he must be convinced that the work in question is ethically right. Such a preoccupation easily makes the critic prejudiced in regard to many other elements in a work, and precludes the possibility of an objective judgment.

The question of objectivity is equally suspected in case of the Impressionists also. They were tempted to explain a literary work on the basis of the effects it had in them. The text to the impressionistic critic was some sort of a stimulus that created various responses in the minds of man. This process of stimulus and response, however, is purely subjective, because the responses were likely to vary from critic to critic. Naturally it tended to become more creative than critical. Mencken in 1919 expressed his view that the critic "makes the work of art live for the spectator; he makes the spectator live for the work of art" (Mencken 21). His suggestion is that a critic should try to be creative. In fact, we find that the text to an impressionist is the starting point as well as the point of departure because the text just triggers off the critic's imagination and he gives us his impressions without assigning any scientific or objective reasons for having those impressions. He does not care to locate in the text the rational sources of his impressions. Thus there remains a great possibility of exaggeration and personal enthusiasm in it and the intellectual side of criticism—the examination of the interior structure and principles of organization in a literary work, and the evaluation of the artistic process—are more or less neglected.

Marxist criticism, immediately after its appearance received enormous attention of the critics and was widely cultured during the thirties. Its earlier stand of course did not remain unchanged. In the hands of the later critics like Jameson, Althusser and Eagleton it has been widely modified; its scope has broadened to accommodate new approaches. However, in general, we may say that "Marxism has shown two faces—a historical method which is analytic, and a doctrinal position which is dogmatic" (Levin 257). The Marxist critics, out of their extreme partiality to the theory of socio-economico-political goal of writing, popularized the view that the social, economic and political values of a literary work must be established first because the artist as an individual is restricted and influenced by those factors of his contemporary life. The real cause of the artistic creation, according to the Marxist critics, can be found in the socio-economico-political factors of that period. Thus, the mistake they make is to reduce the scope of criticism and to keep aside the aesthetic criterion of judging a literary work as a literary work and not as a social document. They fail to realize that the creative mind, though not free from the socio-political influences of its immediate environment, is never engaged in a direct presentation of those factors. If it happened to be so, then journalism could also be literature because it represents the socio-political situation of a period; and the age-old works of literature could no longer please us because the socio-economic situations in which they were written, do not exist today. What all these different groups of literary critics actually fail to notice out of an extreme fascination for their own theories is that poetic or aesthetic practice includes more than one principle, object and idea. Therefore, any method which aims at a single aspect, as most of the available theories do, is sure to be inadequate and incomplete, though not necessarily wrong.

II

The New Criticism, which has of course remarkably great contribution to literary criticism, ultimately falls a victim to the monistic shortcomings. The origin of this critical movement can be traced back to its reaction to Impressionism, Marxist criticism, New Humanism and such other critical theories, which were chiefly extra-textual criticism in the sense that their primary interest was on the elements other than the aesthetic ones. The observation of William Phillips may be cited here. Phillips observes: "The New Criticism was, of course, largely a creation against earlier impressionist and biographical approaches and one dimensional social and historical interpretations of literature, particularly the Marxist variety. It was an attempt to free literature from being a branch of civics or morality or politics" (Phillips 374). In fact, critics did not pay sufficient attention to the texts. And it is primarily as a reaction to this neglect of the texts that the New Critics make the texts the object of first importance in any type of critical evaluation. Eliot may be considered to be the pioneer of this new temperament because he, in 1919, tried "to divert interest from the poet to the poetry" by recommending that "honest criticism and sensitive appreciation is directed not upon the poet but upon the poetry" (Eliot *Tradition* 53 & 59).

The New Criticism has resurrected the text by advocating close reading free from preconceptions and theoretical speculations. One may ask whether it is possible for a critic to approach a work of art with a mind, like a clean slate, free from all preconceptions. But that is a different question. Our point is that the greatest contribution of the New Critics is to emphasize the importance of the text. However, the New Critics unfortunately do not stop there and go to the extreme. They consider the literary text to be an autonomous, self-contained and organic object, having no extra-textual loyalty. Thus, a good many aspect—biographical, historical, sociological and the like—are simply kept aside, drastically reducing the scope of criticism in process. They are concerned chiefly with those aspects which were either neglected or not taken into consideration by the preceding theories of literary criticism. The New Criticism builds its magnificent critical superstructure on the basis of an intensified attention on the previously neglected aesthetic qualities of the literary art. But this new theory also, due to the enthusiastic zeal of its practitioners to make criticism exclusively text-based, neglects the extra-textual aspects, which are not less important to evaluate a work like Shakespeare's *Henry IV* or Dickens' *A Tale of Two Cities*—a work that exploits the social or political history of a land.

The New Critics are chiefly recognized as critics of poetry. But even in that field their theory is incomplete. Cleanth Brooks, for example, concentrates his attention on the pervasive function of paradox. He declares it to be at the centre of all poems. He is of course sensible in his arguments regarding the critical analysis of a poem. He rightly thinks that a poem is a united whole and that the paraphrasing method of analysis leaves hidden the unparaphrasable elements in a poem. But his implication that a simple set of criterion—that is the criterion of paradox is sufficient to judge all types of poetry is hardly acceptable. There are poems—the 19th century romantic poems of Wordsworth and others, for example, which cannot be satisfactorily judged by this single criterion. That is why R.S. Crane reacted so forcefully in his review of Brooks' *The Well Wrought Urn*. And even Ransom, who was one of the great New critics, criticises Brooks' view that poetry is the language of paradox. Simple, sensuous, and passionate poems are actually there which do not depend on paradox for their poetic appeal. Most of the Elizabethan lyrics may exemplify this. Ransom feels that paradox as a principle of poetry is a very weak basis and he prescribes instead a closer attention to structure, giving the superior place to the poetry of things and the inferior to the poetry of ideas. But Ransom here does the same prescriptive fallacy of monistic approach by denouncing the 'paradox' theory of Brooks and prescribing his own method. He fails to realize that the theory of paradox must be helpful in some cases, and therefore it cannot be rejected as totally wrong or useless. He also remains blind to the limitations of his distinction between the poetry of things and the poetry of ideas. For every poem must necessarily contain idea, at least from the poets' point of view. And the 'poetry of idea,' if any poem can be called thus, is never idea alone; objects in some form or other must remain to give a body to the idea. In other words, Ransom fails to understand that the concrete and the abstract in poetry are not mutually exclusive.

Again, Ransom calls the New Criticism as specifically literary criticism, and he maintains that "business of the literary critic is exclusively with an aesthetic criticism" (Ransom 101-02). This view of Ransom is obviously a protest against the Marxist negligence of the aesthetic values. But here he commits the same mistake, like the Marxist critics, of reducing the scope of criticism. A critic is surely not a moralist, or a historian or a sociologist, but why should a critic be disallowed the consideration of the social, historical or other aspects of a literary work? This tendency leads to the contention that the New Critics' view of art was limited as John Fekete has pointed out. He writes, "[...] art must be seen as a moment of the historical practice of the social formation, intimately involved, within the categories of the totalization of praxis, with the essentials of human development at a concrete moment in space and time; and Ransom and the New Critics failed to locate art in these terms" (Fekete 102). The New Critics only emphasized an empiricist close reading of the text but failed to see that it can hardly attain success without, in the language of Frye, "a sense of the archetypal shape of literature as a whole" (Frye 342). In their judgment of a work of art, the New Critics lose the help of the analogies of different literary genres. They approach the various genres like poetry, drama and novel with the same set of criterion, ignoring the fact that every individual branch of literature as a unique mode of discourse possesses certain peculiarities of its own. Such a monistic approach is bound to be partial, and therefore incomplete.

Actually critical monism, the tendency that prevails in most of the critical theories including the New Criticism, is a less effective and less fruitful pursuit because it takes under its consideration only one or two aspects of literature. It never allows a critic to look beyond its limited premises, even when the text may have other aspects to be considered. And this characteristic defect of critical monism is one of the major reasons why a change in critical approach becomes gradually imminent towards the second half of 1940s. A. Walton Litz has carefully marked this change and thus remarked that "the general trend of literary criticism since 1945 has been from consensus to diversity, from the dominance of formalistic criticism to a bewildering variety of criticisms which seek to move 'beyond' or 'against' formalism" (Litz 51). This changing attitude was clear in the rise and writings of the Chicago group of critics headed by R.S. Crane, upon whom the designation of 'pluralistic critic' has been given although, it must be noted, he never used or accepted the term 'pluralism' in its present mistaken sense of a theory of 'live and let live.'

2

Rise of the Chicago School of Criticism

During the thirties and early forties of the 20th century the major "controversy among literary theorists centred chiefly on the 'true' nature of poetry and the 'proper' character of criticism" (Crane *Critics and Criticism* iii). I do not want to generalize or over simplify the complex critical scene of the thirties and early forties. But truly speaking that was, in brief, what the critics of this transitional period had been trying to achieve. The traditions of impressionistic and moralistic criticisms were already estimated to be incomplete and unsatisfactory. The primary enthusiasm of Marxist criticism was also at a low ebb. The new trend in criticism initiated by Eliot and Richards reached its height in the New Criticism. But it has also failed to offer us a method of comprehensive criticism of literary art. Different critics of this group, tend to give us different views of poetry and poetic criticism.

In such a situation the writings of the Chicago group received some attention. Their primary aim was to rectify the deficiencies of all the previous critical theories and to offer a scientific and fruitful method for critical analysis. They do not discard any theory as wrong. They examine the limitations of the past theories—their tendencies of dogmatism and reductionism—and emphasize the necessity of formulating a really fruitful method of critical judgment on the basis of a knowledge of the defects of the preceding theories. Eliseo Vivas, in his review of *Critics and Criticism*, has rightly observed that "Crane and his friends have always put main emphasis on the principles and methods of criticism" (Vivas 137).

The Chicago critics believe, and quite correctly, that the ends or results of one's analysis of a literary work may and do vary as and when the principles applied to the process of analysis are different. This is a part of what Richard Mckeon in his article, "The Philosophical Bases of Art and Criticism," suggests. Mckeon observes that the doctrinal differences are largely due to the differences in principles and their philosophical foundations. Thus, the apparent disagreements among critics are not always real disagreements. They are often results of the potentialities of the critical terms, used in a multiplicity of senses, and also of the philosophical assumptions which determine the different principles of critical analysis.

Crane also supports Mckeon's view when he says that "literary criticism is not and never has been a single discipline, to which successive writers have made partial and never wholly satisfactory contributions, but rather a collection of distinct and more or less incommensurable 'frameworks' or poetic structures which necessarily takes on a different meaning and receives a different kind of answer from the meaning it has and the kind of answer it is properly given in any of the rival critical languages in which it is discussed" (Crane *Languages of Criticism* 13). To illustrate his point Crane mentions the critical war between Bradley and L.C. Knights. It is no war at all. The same subject matter may be approached differently, leading to two different results. Two critics, working with the same subject, namely 'tragedy' or *Macbeth* or 'Shakespearean tragedy' for example, may focus the readers' attention on two different aspects by the semantic and logical constitutions of their discourse. It proves that there are many critical subject matters hidden under the various familiar names for literary entities. All these subjects have their basis in a mysteriously abstract thing like human mind; their characters are always changing and relative, quite different from the invariant natural phenomena.

In his "Questions and Answers in the Teaching of Literary Texts" also Crane exhibits how doctrinal conclusions may and do vary as the contexts in which the critics consider certain problems about the literary texts differ. Crane clearly says that "all statements in criticism have logical contexts, apart from which nothing significant can be said about them; and the immediate context of any statement is the precise question (often not explicitly formulated at all) to which it is an intended answer" (Crane *Humanities* Vol. II 26). So the statement (or answer) in critical observation must differ widely from critic to critic as the contexts (which are questions) differ. What follows then is that we cannot allow a comparative study of doctrinal conclusions of any two critics, and cannot discard one as wrong until we are satisfied that they are answers to the same question. Crane also observes that contexts are relative to the "larger contexts of primary terms, distinctions, and premises which make up the conceptual 'framework' of the critic's writing, and determine both what questions he will think it possible or important to ask and what kinds of answers he will seek for them" (Crane *Humanities* Vol. II 179). When all these will be taken into consideration, it must be found that "what appears to be hopeless doctrinal conflicts in criticism are not really doctrinal conflicts at all, but simply expressions of preference among different, but equally defensible, frameworks, within any two of which the seemingly common referents of the critics' statements may only nominally be the same" (Crane *Humanities* Vol. II 179).

Elder Olson's assumption is also basically the same. The number of critical positions, he thinks, is not one but many. Criticism is a branch of philosophy and, therefore, the number of possible philosophical positions determine the number of possible critical positions. Olson, along with the other Chicagoans, shares the view, as Pritchard points out, that "criticisms differ according as they centre upon one or another facet of art: its medium, its productive cause, its end, or as they focus upon several of these facets at once" (Pritchard 281). Naturally, a particular theory that takes up only one or two of these various facets is incomplete but not conflicting with another theory that considers some others. We should, therefore, Olson concludes, try to achieve a critical method that will allow us to consider all the important aspects of a literary work. It is out of this belief that Olson, at the beginning of his essay "An Outline of Poetic Theory," criticizes and rejects dogmatism, syncretism and scepticism because neither a dogmatist, nor a syncretist, nor even a sceptic realizes that the differences in critical principles and observations are not always real differences. "All these views," Olson observes, "are potentially harmful to learning in so far as, in suppressing discussion, they suppress some (and in the case of scepticism, all) of the problems and because, consequently, they retard or even arrest progress within the subject" (Olson "Poetic Theory" 3).

The Chicagoans, thus, were well aware of two major aspects in framing their critical theory—one is the limitations or the incomplete nature of monistic criticism, and the other is the multiplicity of critical approaches. And this awareness, in fact, led them to hail critical pluralism. But I must hasten to add that the Chicagoans never accepted the term 'pluralism' in its often mistaken sense of a theory of forceful yoking of all the available dogmas. They knew very well that a literary piece may not be fit for all the theories available so far. Naturally, any approach to a literary work with a host of critical dogmas may create only an insensible jumble but no clear critical opinion. It is on this point that Crane specially emphasizes. He, of course, does not exclude dogma from the scope of literary criticism. He rather admits the necessity of some sort of dogma, or 'a set of first principles' in his own words, to start with. But his point is that these 'principles' are to be used not to exclude any of the already existing opinions, but to solve some particular critical problems amenable to solution. The critic is free to use any principle which may seem useful to solve his problems. Thus, what the Chicagoans mean to suggest by critical pluralism is simply that a critic must not work to show the applicability or correctness of his own method; he will rather work to judge and evaluate the literary piece properly, and in this task he may take the help of as many principles as he thinks useful. It will help the critic to evaluate any type of work, changing his principles as the texts will require, and to show the various aspects of a literary work successfully.

Such a concept of criticism, we must note, is not in war with any of the existing critical theories, including the New Criticism. It may really help "an enlargement rather than a further restriction of the sources of criticism" (Crane *Critics and Criticism* vii). That is why A. Walton Litz remarks: "The ideas of Crane and his group may be viewed as complementary to those of such critics as Empson, Brooks, and Blackmur. In contrast to the 'monism' of many of his contemporaries, Crane saw himself as a 'pluralist,' trying to recognize the virtues of different critical and scholarly method and their appropriateness to the literary problem at hand" (Litz 59). It may also be recalled in this context that what Frederick A. Pottle says in *The Idiom of Poetry* about the philosophy of critical relativism is undoubtedly a support of the pluralistic view of criticism. Pottle observes that standards are variable and that the judgments a critic passes are always relative to the age in which they are made. Tastes change sharply and there is no reason for "concluding that taste grows progressively better, or that the mere passage of time widens literary sympathies and sharpens the critical faculty" (Pottle 28-29). What follows from Pottle's observation is that each critic is right (though he may be limited) in so far as he approaches his standards of judgment consistently. But he must be wrong if he insists that his methods and, consequently, his judgments are absolute and infallible—true for all time. He is actually required, as and when necessary, to change the means and principles for dealing with different critical problems.

The pluralistic ideal of the Chicagoans, however, should not create the mistaken impression in anybody that this group of critics has no distinctive method of criticism, and that they only impart on us the knowledge of the applicability of different critical theories to different critical problems. Pritchard commits this mistake when he says that "the study of criticism as they [the Chicago critics] envisage it is not designed to develop any new or peculiar critical method, but to examine and evaluate those approaches to literature which have been or currently are being used for its interpretation and judgment. Their work includes therefore the criticism of criticism" (Pritchard 280). The mistake Pritchard commits here is simply that he misunderstands pluralism as a way of trying various critical theories to a literary work. The Chicagoans, as has already been seen, never use the term in that sense. They have followed a particular method of critical analysis which, they think, will be free from the limitations of a monistic approach and will, at the same time, enable us to have a harmonious and comprehensive criticism of literary works.

The critical method which the Chicagoans offer us may be, in a very general way, called a formal or structural approach to literature. They believe that a literary work "like any other production of human art, has, or rather is, a definite structure of some kind which is determined immediately by its writer's intuition of a form to be achieved in its materials by the right use of his medium" (Crane *Languages of Criticism* 165). The task will be to realize the particular form of a literary work, and on the basis of his understanding he will select some specific principles of analysis. The principles thus may and do vary from work to work. And it is in this point that the Chicagoans differ from the New Critics even when they, like the New Critics, concentrate upon a poem as a poem primarily, and judge a poem upon its intrinsic merits. They never believe that a single criterion or principle is adequate to judge works of all the varieties. Pritchard rightly says that "far from proclaiming a new critical panacea the Chicago critics urge the application to literature of varied critical procedures" (Pritchard 281-82). They, unlike the New Critics, consider the critical principles not as doctrinal absolutes but as instruments of analysis.

To a Chicago critic a poem or a literary work is a distinctive whole, which has its own unique function in human experience. And criticism, to them, is a reasoned discourse. Both the concepts make the Chicagoans Aristotelian in some respect. Actually Aristotle is there "behind what they [the Chicago critics] have sought to do in many of their essays in poetic theory and practical criticism" (Crane *Critics* iv). But this by no way means that they are dogmatic supporters of Aristotle and his approach. Crane has clearly said that "they have been greatly interested, all along in the particular class of critical problems which Aristotle was the first, possibly the last, to discuss systematically, and for the study of which he evolved an appropriate and workable method" (Crane *Critics* iii). And, therefore, they tried to "pursue similar lines of study in the poetics of modern literature" (Crane *Critics* iii). They have thus enlarged and modified the Aristotelian approach through additions and alterations in the light of the literary needs of the century. They are thus 'neo-Aristotelian' in a very restricted sense, because they never support Aristotle blindly. Crane's "our loyalty at any rate should be to problems rather than to ancient masters" (Crane *Languages* 149) sounds like a warning to themselves and to the succeeding generations of critics. In other words, Crane warns us against a dogmatic following of Aristotle. At the same time he suggests that we should not hesitate to take help of his insights if we face such problems in an analysis and understanding of literary texts. It will almost be the same as our contemporary critics benefit from the observations of Freud, Jung, Frazer and such others. The Chicagoans, it is remarkable, oppose some earlier Aristotelians who sought to extend Aristotle's observations on tragedy to other literary genres. The Chicagoans stand aloof from this group due to their belief, in a purely Aristotelian strain, that "each literary genre has its own principles of construction, and poems achieve wholeness by conforming to the principles of their genres" (Pritchard 281).

It will not be irrelevant now to point out some of the concepts in which the Chicagoans differ from the New Critics. It has already been observed that the Chicago critics support the New Critics' concentration on literary texts, their consideration of literary work as primarily a work of art as well as their emphasis on the formal aspect of poetry or literature. But the Chicagoans do not support the New Critics' view about the ends of poetry. The ends of poetry to the New Critics are a superior kind of knowledge. And in support of their theory the New Critics often cite those lines from the *Poetics* where Aristotle, while speaking about history and poetry, declares the "one (history) describes the thing that has been, and the other (poetry) a kind of thing that might be. Hence poetry is something more philosophic and of graver import than history, since its statements are of the nature rather of universals, whereas those of history are singulars" (Aristotle 43). The Chicago critics, on the contrary, believe that 'pleasure,' not 'knowledge' is the end for which a literary work primarily exists. The construction of work with a specific form, having organic unity of its parts produces the pleasure specific to its form. This difference between the Chicago and the New Critics in regard to the 'end' of poetry signifies the necessary difference between their respective attitudes to a literary work. Knowledge as an end of poetry requires an evaluative judgment of the nature and value of poetry or any other form of literary works, whereas the other concept—the concept of pleasure as the end—refers to the basic structural principle in every composition.

The New Critics adopted a method of verbal analysis based on the formal and linguistic aspects of a work of art. The Chicagoans think that it makes the New Critics psychologistic in their approach. The same set of words may convey meanings and suggestions of different kinds. Naturally, then, a verbal analysis can hardly lead to the same judgment regarding a literary work. Different critics arrive at different critical judgments of the same work. The Chicago critics, therefore, follow the method of structural analysis on the basis of the formal principles of the literary artists. This, they think, will maintain a uniformity of critical observations.

Differences between the two groups are also there in regard to their ideas about certain Aristotelian terms like 'plot,' 'catharsis' etc. The Chicago critics use the word 'plot' not to mean, as it is often used to mean at present, the story element of a work. In their concept it is a framework or a means to an end. The elements of character, thought, action etc., out of which the artist effects a temporal synthesis are only the contents of a plot but not the plot proper. Plot is something for the Chicagoans which fashions the material objects of a work (character, action, thought, diction etc.) into a definite artistic object. And the excellence of a plot "depends upon the power of its peculiar synthesis of character, action and thought, as inferable from the sequence of words, to move out feelings powerfully and pleasurably in a certain definite way" (Crane *Critics* 68). To the Chicagoans, therefore, plot is of great importance—almost the soul of a work.

But the New Critics believe in the pre-eminence of language or words rather than that of plot. In their view the words are important because they are the limit of what the poet has to say. To the Chicagoans, however, it is not the words actually, but what they stand for, that is important. And they think that the New Critics' dogmatic adherence to language is a severe limitation of their method.

Before I pass on to an observation of the theoretical appliances of R.S. Crane in the following chapter, it is necessary, I think, to consider one more point—the point of René Wellek's criticism of the Chicagoans' 'ideals of complete objectivity.' René Wellek, I think, has not properly followed the theoretical stand of the Chicago school of critics when he says that "the Chicago group are learned historian of criticism with the impractical ideals of complete objectivity and completeness of evidence" (Wellek 66). Ray also made a similar point as early as in 1984 in the 16th Triennial Congress of the International Federation of Modern Languages and Literatures, held in Budapest, 1984, when he remarked, "[...] since man is a man, and not a machine, he can never attain scientific objectivity in relation to a work of art, as his judgment on it has to depend on his reaction to it. Moreover the personality of one critic will always differ from that of another critic by virtue of his experiences, knowledge and belief" (Ray "Change in Language and Literature" 287). The Chicagoans no doubt valued objectivity in criticism, and there can be no dispute in the fact that any responsible criticism requires objective analysis of a literary work. But since the mind is involved in the act of analysis and evaluation, and since the critic is not a machine but man, absolute objectivity can never be attainable perhaps in practice. The Chicagoans, in fact, never aspire for such an unattainable mechanical objectivity. Crane, for example, has elaborated his idea of objectivity in criticism in many of his essays. He has repeatedly suggested that a critic should try to be as objective as possible. The method of hypothesis making, which Crane illustrates in his essay "On Hypothesis in Historical Criticism," may be cited as an example of how he tries to make a critic more objective and unbiased in his judgment. This is never a sign of the "impractical ideals of complete objectivity" as Wellek complains.

The same thing can be said about what Wellek calls the Chicagoans' desire for a 'completeness of evidence.' The Chicago critics, in order that rash, subjective judgments may be avoided, have emphasized that a critic's observation about a literary work must conform to all the internal and external aspects of that work. If any aspect of the text disagrees with the critic's findings, one may suspect the validity of them. Such an attitude of the Chicagoans, if seen in proper perspective and spirit, appears to be quite reasonable and it goes a long way in forming a tradition of responsible criticism. Such an ideal will make a critic more careful in the selection of his hypothesis as well as in passing his final comments on a literary work.

The Chicago school of critics, thus, appears at a time when literary criticism through a long tradition of monistic approach became extremely limited. They surely broaden the scope of criticism by pointing out the limitations of monism, and also by showing the way toward a more liberal, more comprehensive form of criticism in which the unhealthy rivalry of *-isms* does not exist.

3

Crane's Theoretical Appliances

R.S. Crane, the leader of the Chicago school of critics and an editor of *Modern Philology* for some twenty years, drew enormous attention of critics, scholars and theorists after the publication of *Critics and Criticism* (1952) and *The Languages of Criticism and the Structure of Poetry* (1953). In fact, Crane and his followers assembled at the University of Chicago sometime in the mid 1930s and had been publishing their critical contributions in various journals, but it was only after the publication of these volumes that they could exert "a strong and continuing influence on modern criticism" (Fowler *Dictionary* 29). These books, especially the second one, illustrates Crane's theory of criticism on a much broader and more humane perspective. Crane studies literature as an integral part of a larger problem of human education and considers criticism as essentially a branch of philosophy. For every kind of criticism, he thinks, there is a philosophical foundation to draw sustenance from, and the number of critical positions is, therefore, determined by the number of possible philosophical positions. This belief makes Crane aware of an existence of the multiplicity of critical languages or frameworks, and in order to have best results out of this situation Crane, the theorist, proposes a theory of critical pluralism. The particular subject with reference to which he elaborates his theory is the structure of poetry. However, Crane uses the word poetry in this context more or less in the Aristotelian sense to mean any artistic creation in words. He examines the critical frameworks of Aristotle, and of the moderns to show how the structure of poetry receives different forms and significations in different critical frameworks and finally he gives his own theory which he considers to be a more comprehensive scheme of critical analysis.

I

There are critics, Crane observes, like Aristotle who believe in a multiplicity of poetic structures. Side by side there are others like Cleanth Brooks who are of the opinion that the essential structure of poetry is one. Thus they form two different groups of critics having two essentially different attitudes to the problem of poetic structure. Again critics of any of these two groups widely vary among themselves in respect of their individual theorizing. Each critic seems to differ from others in respect of what he says about the structure of an individual poem, no matter whether he believes in the multiplicity or singleness of structure. The reasons behind such wide disagreements can be found in an analysis of critical propositions framed by various critics.

The character of a critical proposition should be determined by three independently variable factors. One factor is the critic himself as a man equipped with certain range of information, intellectual capacity and a certain kind of taste and sensibility. Another factor is the concrete literary object or the text upon which he is engaged. And a third factor is the power and limitation of the discourse which the critic constructs. Every critic uses a particular framework of selected terms and distinctions and of rules for operating with them with a view to interpreting the text in hand. This 'framework' or a particular type of critical language gives sense to a critic's observations. A critic cannot step beyond his immediate framework and, naturally, cannot consider those aspects or sides of a literary production, which do not come within the capacity or the framework he happens to choose. "We are thus," Crane observes, "in all our inquiries into things, the more or less willing and productive prisoners of the special system of 'language' we have chosen to employ; it is only in relation to this system that we can assert anything as a meaningful 'fact' or give determinate significance to any question we ask; and our problems and solutions will differ widely, even when the ostensible subjects remain the same, according to the peculiar conceptual and logical constitution of the 'framework' we happen to be using" (Crane *Languages* 12). So this third factor is equally important as the two others, and the differences in critical propositions are largely due to the differences of frameworks.

Generally, critical problems are solved and principles derived by means of two different and contrasting methods. In the first method, which Crane calls 'the matter of fact criticism,' the critic seeks to present an account of empirically distinguishable literary phenomena in terms of their essential and distinctive causes of production. For instance, a tragedy in this method is taken as a particular type of artistic production having as its distinctive features a particular plot form, character treatment and such other aspects devised in a manner to arouse a specific response. In the other method some abstract principles are at first framed and then applied to the subject in question. Crane calls it abstract criticism. Tragedy in this method may be taken "as the name of a universal attitude or 'vision' of life, the distinctive nature of which is defined in a dialectical opposition to another similarly universal attitude or vision of life for which the word 'comedy' is thought to be the appropriate symbol" (Crane *Languages* 25). Critics generally follow either of these two methods. And the important point is that the nature of propositions may and does vary as the one or the other method is taken up. It proves what Crane finds that "literary criticism is not and never has been a single discipline to which successive writers have made partial and never wholly satisfactory contributions but rather a collection of distinct and more or less incommensurable 'frameworks' or 'languages,' within any one of which a question like that of poetic structure necessarily takes on a different meaning and receives a different kind of answer from the meaning it has and the kind of answer it is properly given in any of the rival critical languages in which it is discussed" (Crane *Languages* 13).

In such a situation of the multiplicity of critical frameworks Crane intends to offer us the most fruitful method of critical interpretation. And he proposes the theory of critical pluralism, which, however, is different from what either S.E. Hyman or R.P. Blackmur suggests. S.E. Hyman and a few other critics yearn for a 'synthesis' of various critical doctrines. The job of an ideal critic, he thinks, should be to combine in his work the best insights and techniques of the large variety of critics. And Blackmur's suggestion is that the only possible way to remove the narrowness of contemporary criticism is to make possible an 'alliance' between different sorts of critics, say, Aristotle and Coleridge. He tells us to collect the important aspects from both Aristotle and Coleridge together. The result, he thinks, will be better than either of the critics taken separately. Both Hyman and Blackmur fail to realize the actual nature of the problem, and their suggestions, therefore, can hardly solve the problem of varying critical doctrines. What Hyman suggests is merely to make a list of critical insights and techniques. Such a list may only help us giving ready-made information about critical solutions. And Blackmur's theory of 'alliance' is not a theory at all. It leaves us no scope to identify the virtues of an individual critic.

Crane's theory of critical pluralism is different from the theory of either Hyman or Blackmur. It stands in sharp contrast with the monistic tendency to assert any particular theory as the only correct and profitable one. The pluralistic critic, Crane informs us, "would take the view that the basic principles and methods of any distinguishable mode of criticism are tools of inquiry and interpretation rather than formulations of the 'real' nature of things and that the choice of any special 'language,' among the many possible for the study of poetry, is a practical decision to be justified solely in terms of the kind of knowledge the critic wants to attain" (Crane *Languages* 31). He will be aware of the fact that most of the differences in critical propositions are due to the differences in critical frameworks, and that various critical theories are different but not mutually exclusive. Naturally, even the most diverse sort of proposition must be judged in terms of the framework in which it occurs. And thus considered, a pluralistic critic will easily get the help of a large number of critical insights, which will enable him to form a more comprehensive approach to literary problems.

To accept most of the critical pronouncements as relevant, however, is by no means to suggest that there will remain no standard for distinguishing the good critical performances from the bad ones. We can, Crane suggests, make comparative evaluations among the different existing languages of criticism. We may also judge if a critic, in his act of interpretation, violates the accepted canons of reasoning, hypothesis-making and of common-sense. He must also be true to the literary text he considers.

These, then, are the major philosophical assumptions upon which Crane founds his actual theory of critical analysis. But before analysing the method of critical interpretation that Crane expresses in terms of an examination of the structure of poetry and which he considers to be the most effective method, it will be relevant, I think, to analyse briefly what Crane observes about the result of an examination of the structure of poetry in the 'languages' or critical frameworks of Aristotle and the moderns.

II

Aristotle, Crane observes, unlike almost any other philosopher considering poetic art seriously, believed in a theory of the multiplicity of linguistic systems. Plato, for instance, used the same system of language for the discussion of both poetry and music. He of course treated the two subjects differently, but the language of his discussion is essentially the same. Other philosophers like Hume, Hobbes, Hegel and Croce also take help more or less of a single language to discuss both poetry and other arts in themselves as well as in relation to other things. But Aristotle believed that every distinguishable thing, such as poetry, presents a multiplicity of aspects and relations, each one of which may be examined in different languages or critical frameworks. And in his own practice Aristotle is found to use different system of language and principles for talking about poetry, for example, in his different treatises—on poetry, on ethics, on politics and the like. Thus, while in *Politics* Aristotle is concerned with efficient causes in relation to the good of citizens, in *Poetics* it is the intrinsic good in relation to the art of the poet. It will be a mistake, Crane warns, to understand and consider them in the same way. The validity of a statement can be determined only by its proper contextualization.

Crane explains the major assumptions upon which Aristotle bases the line of inquiry he pursues in the *Poetics*, and these assumptions, Crane thinks, give him the basic framework of his analysis. Naturally, the critical propositions which Aristotle has offered become meaningful only when they are considered in relation to the framework within which they occur. Crane mentions three major assumptions. Firstly, Aristotle thinks that "the primary concern of poetics will not be with the actual process of poetic creation but rather with the poetic reasoning—from the character of the end to be achieved to the necessary or desirable means that is reflected in this process when it terminates in an artistically successful product" (Crane *Languages* 46). For, the actual poetic process may vary from artist to artist but poetic reasoning or the conception of the type of poetry artists are engaged to compose is more or less the same. In other words, the structural parts of a particular type of work will more or less be the same even when the artists may differ in respect of the particular process they follow to arrange and employ those parts. Secondly, poetics will deal with necessities of two kinds—those which form the essential conditions or parts of all poems and those others which are specific to different poetic forms. What follows from this is that poetics must present a causal analysis of the various poetic species which differ from one another in order to show the necessities which are peculiar to each of the various poetic species. Thirdly, the end of all inquiries of poetics, since it is treated as a practical science, "must be the discovery of what is the best possible state, consistent with their specific natures, to which different kinds of poems and their parts may be brought" (Crane *Languages* 47). These three major assumptions, it is needless to repeat, give Aristotle the basic framework or language of his inquiry. And Crane points out some of the special features of this critical framework.

Aristotle, as has already been suggested, aims at composing a productive science of poetry having as its primary subject-matter the various necessities involved in the making of poetic wholes of one or another specific kind. His problem therefore, Crane observes, in what he likes to perform is twofold. In the first place he has to define particular species of poetry from their existing varieties and at the same time has to point out the nature and number of the constituent parts of each of the species as well as its various subspecies. In the second place he is required to point out the conditions of artistic success and failure of the poetic forms he chooses to consider. Aristotle believes that "every art and every inquiry and similarly every action and pursuit, is thought to aim at some good" (Aristotle 1-2). So he is also required to clarify the nature of the 'good' or the end of poetry as well as the 'good' which poetics must aim at achieving. And in the *Poetics* , one must agree, Aristotle does all these things quite systematically. Only what we must remember is that Aristotle is concerned mainly with tragedy—which is only one of the many existing forms of poetry; he does not offer us a theory of poetry in general. And Crane's claim is that if we read the *Poetics* as an attempt to deal with a particular type of poetry, and not as an attempt to form the poetics of all kinds of poetry, we may immensely benefit from Aristotle's observations as well as of his method of analysis.

III

The critical language of our contemporary critics, Crane observes, are remarkably different from those of either Aristotle or other critics of the past though they can hardly deny the influences of various critical languages of the past. Aristotle, for instance, influences the later generations of critics in two major forms. Firstly, it has been an influence of and upon doctrine. Aristotle's critical statements about various aspects like catharsis, tragic hero etc. have been interpreted, through ages, in various ways, on the basis of which the *Poetics* has sometimes been invoked and sometimes repudiated. Secondly, the influence of Aristotle is quite obvious in the fact that critics are often found to exploit purely Aristotelian terms like 'action,' 'character,' 'plot,' 'thought' etc. even in their attempts to frame critical observations in a way which is absolutely un-Aristotelian. But these two types of influences are far from making the critical languages of the later critics identical with the language of Aristotle, because a critical language is "something more fundamental than the particular doctrinal conclusions it is used to express and the particular terminology in which its analysis is stated" (Crane *Languages* 80). The more important or inner aspect of Aristotle's treatise—the principle or method that acts as a guiding force in Aristotle—is not found to be properly adopted by his successors. The approach of the later critics to poetry was basically different from that of Aristotle.

The modern critics, unlike Aristotle, have defined poetry in general. For them poetry is sometime 'statement' (as in Winters), or 'communication' (as in Brooks and Warren), or 'knowledge' (as in Prof. Pottle). It must, however, be mentioned here that Crane cites from Yvor Winters' *The Anatomy of Nonsense* to show that for Winters poetry is a statement in words. But Winters modified his definition of poetry in his later books. He says, "I use the term 'statement' in a very inclusive sense, and for a lack of something better" (Winters *Function* 26). In another book also he says, "A poem is first of all a statement in words. But it differs from all such statements of a purely philosophical or theoretical nature, in that, it has by intention a controlled content of feeling" (Winters *Defence* 363). It will thus be a mistake to understand 'statement' in the ordinary sense of the term. However, all the modern critics more or less take it for granted that the term 'poetry' refers to one qualitatively homogeneous thing, however variously it may manifest itself in the various poetic genres. Another important point that Crane has mentioned is that in the moderns the individual works or group of works are determined as 'poem' only after giving the definitions of poetry, whereas in Aristotle they exist as concrete objects (with which the *Poetics* deals), prior to the inquiry into their nature.

Unfortunately Crane does not distinguish between 'poetry' and 'poem.' The modern critics that he has cited have given definitions of poems and hinted at what poetry is like. Poetry is abstract; a poem is a concrete whole. Poetry, therefore, can never be defined the way a poem can be.

However, poetry for the modern critics, as not for Aristotle, exists in a 'verbal universe.' And this very fact, Crane observes, is there at the basis of the principles discovered and applied to examine poetry by the modern critics. The principles of poetics for Aristotle are peculiar to the art of poetry. In his conception they are identical with the necessary and sufficient internal causes or principles of construction that operate in the composition of a poem and make it a beautiful whole of a specific kind. And these principles in Aristotle vary as the species of poetry vary. The principles of poetics for the modern critics, on the contrary, who believe that poetry is essentially a particular type of discourse, are necessarily specifications of principles operative throughout the field of writing as a whole. Their basic principles of poetry are identical with the basic principles of all varieties of verbal composition. And the most basic principles are derived from just two elements, which are essential to any purposive speech—the elements of thing and language, or in other words, those of content and verbal form. These elements, however, are not discovered by the moderns. Crane rightly observes that they are what Quintilian long ago mentioned as *res* and *verba*. Thus, this approach which may rightly be called non-Aristotelian is not so modern as it is often thought to be; its root can be traced back to the classical past—to the grammatical and rhetorical studies of literary texts that started in the schools of Hellenistic Greece. The approach has remained the same in essentials, but it has admitted of several changes or modifications in respect of outlook and terms exploited to study literary texts in various ages. And these modifications have given birth to various slightly different critical languages.

The modern critics believe that poetry is a special kind of language used to express thoughts which are impossible to express in other medium. And the business of the critic is to make clear the nature of this language. Their approach may, therefore, broadly be called semantic which, according to Crane, is the latest version of the Hellenistic-Roman subjection of poetics to grammar and rhetoric. The criticism of this sort deals primarily with words and meanings, images and concepts, symbols and referents, with the help of which poets are supposed to constitute the special kind of the language of poetry. And Crane has pointed out—and this is highly original—that although this approach (the semantic approach) seems to enjoy a striking unity of spirit and method, a close study may discover "beneath the common preoccupation of these critics with 'language,' 'symbol' and 'meaning,' at least two distinctive ways, which are often associated in individual critics, of getting at the semantic nature of poetry and hence of defining the characteristic symbolic structures that condition its meanings and values" (Crane *Languages* 100). These two different ways within the same approach constitute two distinctive contemporary critical languages.

In the first way, which is followed by such eminent critics as I.A. Richards, William Empson, Wilson Knight, J.C. Ransom, R.P. Blackmur, Allen Tate and Cleanth Brooks, the language of poetry is, generally speaking, considered as statements in words. And the initial problem of the critics is to differentiate this language of poetry from other modes of verbal discourse. They proceed, as Crane says, "by fixing upon some familiar type of verbal expression which is admittedly not poetry and then deriving the distinctive attributes and structural patterns of poetry by dialectical comparison and contrast with this" (Crane *Languages* 100). The critics, thus, preoccupy themselves primarily with the negative analogies between the verbal aspect of poetry and those of science or prose. And so far as the unity and structure of poetry are concerned these critics try to find out the dominant 'attitude' to which all the other thematic elements of a particular poem appear to conform.

The structure of poetry in this approach may be examined in two different but complementary ways. In one way critics may concentrate on the particular manner or technique used in poetry, as distinct from other modes, to apprehend and express meanings. In it, thus, the critic's primary concern will be with the various elements of poetry like rhythm, diction, imagery, symbols, and such others which cooperate in a particular fashion in each individual poem to express and to give force to what the poet tries to say in the poem. In one sense this type of criticism may almost be similar to the formal criticism. But the essential difference is that the elements of poetry in this criticism, unlike those in formal criticism, are treated not as structural parts but as carriers of meanings. Brooks and Warren, Crane has rightly observed, in *Understanding Poetry* have made this method sufficiently familiar to us.

Another way complementary to the first one is to concentrate on the meanings of the poems themselves, not, as it is in the other way, on the technique or manner of meaningful expressions. The critics, Crane observes, reduce the concrete elements of symbols, images, diction and rhythm to some underlying themes or meanings which those elements are considered to embody. A number of New Critics of Shakespeare like Wilsom Knight, Harold Goddard, Robert Heilman, and Brooks and Warren in some of their later writings have followed this way of interpretation. In his *The Well Wrought Urn*, for example, Brooks finds the inner symbolism of *Macbeth* in the recurrent images which relate on the one hand to the clothes and on the other to young and innocent children. Brooks, Crane thinks, has "generalized from them a pervasive opposition between 'the over-brittle rationalism on which Macbeth founds his career' and the 'irrational' forces in life which Macbeth and Lady Macbeth have left out of account in their conspiracy to capture 'the future' for themselves" (Crane *Languages* 120). My point is that Brooks derives the symbolic structure of *Macbeth* from a consideration mainly of the elements of imagery and diction.

The second of the two contemporary approaches to criticism is popularly called archetypal criticism, and it finds its expression in the works of critics like Maud Bodkin, Kenneth Burke, Edmund Wilson, Lionel Trilling and Northrop Frye. Critics in this approach try to interpret poetry in terms of something else which is considered to be basic in human experience and nature. This other something is either psychology or anthropology, or a combination of both in varying proportions. Actually this approach is based on the achievements in the fields of two non-literary disciplines—the cultural anthropology of Sir James Frazer, Jane Harrison, Emile Durkheim and others, and the analytical psychology of Sigmund Freud and C.G. Jung. These movements had a great influence on this group of critics, poetry for whom is a sort of symbolic language which has close affinities both of nature and of origin with dreams and other psychic manifestations as well as with folk tales and rituals. The starting point of criticism in this approach is not the nature of poetry, but the nature of the universal symbolic process. Consequently, the critical language of this group consists of terms mainly psychological and anthropological.

The structure of poetry to the archetypal critics is more or less identical with the structure of a dream, having at least two levels. And what a critic of this group actually does to expose the structure of an individual poem is, at the first level, to discover the particular archetype which is there in the poem. Mr. Colin Still thus, Crane observes, finds *The Tempest* to have "the double theme of purgation from sin and of rebirth and upward spiritual movement after sorrow and death" (Crane *Languages* 132). Still discovers the 'rebirth archetype' in *The Tempest*, which he thinks gives the basic meaning and structure to the work. At the second level the critic draws an analogy between the archetype discovered in a particular work and the work itself in order to convince the readers that the structure and meaning of the work bear similarities to those of the archetype.

Crane's significant contribution lies in his fine distinction between two major critical frameworks of contemporary criticism: symbolic structure and archetypal pattern. While the symbolic structure is explored from within through an examination of various structural elements, the archetypal pattern is discovered through an affinity between the archetypes used in a poem and the universal archetypes. What is important is that both these conceptions make enough room for multiple interpretations of a literary work—interpretations which are not mutually exclusive.

Crane's observation that the two contemporary approaches to criticism are part of the long tradition of literary criticism which has its origin in the Hellenistic-Roman schools of criticism is important and highly original. It suggests an important aspect which is that the so-called 'New Criticism' is not so new as it often claims to be. A very old tradition of poetic criticism, through modifications and changes, has finally emerged as New Criticism in our century. But to say this is not to minimize by any means the achievements of the New Criticism. What I want to suggest is that Crane's observation actually links this great critical movement of this century to one of the greatest traditions of literary criticism. However, Crane has expressed his dissatisfaction with the critical languages of the moderns as well as with their power of investigation into the nature of the poetic structure of individual poems. He gives, as I shall show in the next section, reasons for his dissatisfaction, and offers us his own theory of critical analysis.

IV

Crane considers the critical languages of the moderns inadequate. In order to determine the adequacy of a procedure in practical criticism, he observes, we must take into account the concepts and modes of reasoning which that particular procedure presupposes. We must also see if that procedure can effectively examine all the important aspects of a literary object it takes into its consideration. If any important aspect is left out of account we may suspect the adequacy of that procedure. Crane's impression is that the two contemporary critical languages, when their adequacy is judged in this scale, are proved to be inadequate, because they do not provide us with any "means for dealing precisely and particularly with [...] the forming principle or immediate shaping cause of structure in individual poems" (Crane *Languages* 140).

What Crane suggests by 'the forming principle' or 'immediate shaping cause' is that there always remains in the artists' mind an 'intuition of a form' which directs him in what he does with the materials of a work. This 'intuition of form,' however, is not thinking, or planning, or incubation, or anything an artist does at the preparatory stage of his writing. From his own experience as an essayist Crane has mentioned that sometimes even after a long and interested concentration on a subject and after collecting all the exciting ideas and patterns of key terms he had to face a lot of troubles to write down even the very first sentence of his essay, whereas, at some other times, he happened to write a whole essay without any trouble or occasional interval even when he was not completely prepared to compose that. What Crane means to suggest here is that there remains something beyond the conscious efforts of an artist which controls his immediate act of construction. This 'something' is, according to Crane, an idea about the particular form which the completed literary work will finally take. The form remains there in the mind of the artist directing him, even though he may hardly be conscious of it, in the act of his actual construction of the artistic whole. This impression of Crane, I think, may help us to understand his stand as a formalist critic. As a formalist Crane gives primacy to form (in this precise sense) over content. He thinks that an artist, even when the content (theme or other materials) is ready in his hand, can hardly construct a successful poetic or artistic whole out of his materials unless the intuition of form is there in his mind as the immediate shaping cause.

The word 'form,' is thus used by Crane in a constructive sense, and he considers that 'form' is an indispensable first principle for every writer. So in practical criticism also this may and should be taken as the first principle of the critic. But unfortunately the two modern approaches to literary works as well as the long tradition of criticism wherefrom the modern approaches have emerged are not found to do this. Actually it was not possible for them to take this particular aspect of form as the first principle in their criticism for two major reasons.

In the first place the critical language in which the contemporary critics have attempted to explain the structures of poetry lack appropriate terms required to explain the 'formal principles' of the artists. They have attempted to deal with the problems of poetic structure on the basis of their assumptions of the non-formal aspects of poetry such as subject-matter or theme, language, and technical procedures. They, thus, concentrate their attention on the various 'patterns' used in the poems, but "they provide no means since none are available in the critical language these critics are using, for helping us to understand why the 'patterns' are there or what their precise function is" (Crane *Languages* 141).

The second important reason why modern critics cannot make the 'formal principle' of a poet the first principle of their criticism is, Crane thinks, that these critics in their concerns for structure in practical criticism start with some predetermined ideas of poetic structure. They usually come to a poem with some sort of a definite specification about the nature of the structural patterns they ought to look for. Thus, the critic who describes poetry as paradox, approaches a poem with the determination of discovering paradox. But no such predetermination, Crane suggests, is possible about the 'formal principle' or 'the shaping cause' of a poem. The critic must discover the formal principle from the particular poem he examines by means of his general concepts. And unless and until he discovers the formal principle that enables an artist to synthesize his materials into an artistic whole, the critic can hardly achieve success in analysing the structure, which is the outcome of that formal principle. The languages of the moderns allow to deal only with the various aspects of poetic structure, not with the causes.

This observation leads Crane to call the modern critical languages inadequate. One may here suspect that Crane contradicts his own belief as a pluralist. As a pluralist Crane hardly discards any approach or theory; he rather bears a free mind to accept the positive values of each and every theory. Here also Crane does not contradict his belief simply because he does neither call the critical languages of the moderns wrong, nor discard them. He only suggests that these languages are not adequate because they cannot give us a comprehensive criticism of the structure of poetry. Therefore, he feels the necessity of a different and we may say developed kind of language for a comprehensive criticism of poetic structure. And he thinks that the critical language of Aristotle can serve this purpose to a great extent.

Crane has given a list of concepts, methods and approaches derived from Aristotle's observations in the *Poetics*, showing how they may help us to solve satisfactorily some of our problems in practical criticism. Crane however leaves the mark of his free mind when he says that "our loyalty at any rate should be to problems rather than to ancient masters" (like Aristotle) (Crane *Languages* 149). In other words, Crane means to suggest that we need not (and also should not) be 'Aristotelian' in a narrow sense of the term, and at the same time we should not hesitate to take any help from Aristotle if we find that we may benefit from his insights in solving some of the problems we face. It will almost be the same as our contemporary critics benefit from the observations of Freud, Jung, Frazer and others.

The first thing that we can have from Aristotle is his concept of poetic works as 'concrete wholes.' A concrete whole, as Crane understands, is something the unity of which can be clearly and adequately stated in terms of the particular 'form' and matter' it employs. The two aspects, 'form' and 'matter,' must join in such a whole, but the form is more important because it is the principle or the cause that gives a definite shape to the 'matter.' Crane illustrates the point with the help of an example. A lump of clay, he says, which is the 'matter' may be given different shapes according to the creator's notion of different particular forms. Matter is thus, in Crane's view, dependent on form for a definite shape. Naturally, in order to understand how form and matter are related in a poem, one must first take into account the formal nature of that poem.

The second important thing, according to Crane, is Aristotle's method of investigation and reasoning. The concept of literary works as concrete wholes gives us a notion about the basic structural relations in a poem. Aristotle framed his method of investigation and reasoning with that notion in mind. The very concept of literary works as concrete wholes organized by formal principles suggests that the critic's problem is to analyse the various elements and subordinate structures of a particular literary work in the light of the particular organizing form of that work. Aristotle's method, Crane suggests, enables a critic, on the one hand, to realize the different forms that can go with different matters, and, on the other, to know the different elements or parts of construction that are essential for giving a body to some particular form.

A few other terms and concept may also help us. But Crane clearly warns—and this is highly significant to indicate Crane's undogmatic stand as a critical theorist—that we must not be satisfied with what we can extract from Aristotle, because the observations of Aristotle—what we get from him in the form of methods and conceptions—cannot satisfactorily explain all the different structural problems which modern works contain. Aristotle considered only that variety of poetry which is imitation, but there are the great varieties of non-imitative species of poetry about which Aristotle said nothing. Even if we talk about the imitative form of poetry we find that Aristotle deals elaborately with only one plot-form which he calls tragic. But there are many other plot forms which we may and do come across in novels and modern plays about which Aristotle had no scope to talk about. Crane's suggestion, therefore, is that a fresh attempt is necessary for a theoretical analysis, in Aristotelian method, of all the different varieties of structures we meet at present. This implies another important thing which is that poetics is an on-going process. It is not something fixed and determined. New kinds of literature will call for new poetics, or an enlargement of the existing one in order to illustrate the functioning of the new literary works.

I may now, when some of Crane's major theoretical concepts have been discussed, illustrate his theory of structural analysis. He has quite categorically shown what the critic, whose intention is to explore the shaping principles of poetic works, is required to do. The critic need not have a thorough knowledge of the variant apparently inconsistent theories of poetry; he need not care for the difference of poetry from other verbal discourses; he need not even worry much about the end of poetry. But the important assumption which the critic must possess is that "any poetic work, like any other production of human art, has, or rather is, a definite structure of some kind which is determined immediately by its writer's intuition of a form to be achieved in its materials by the right use of his medium" (Crane *Languages* 165). He will, therefore, try to understand what this form actually is, and his knowledge or understanding will be used as a principle in the analysis of that work.

Crane believes that a poem with all its material objects like words, images, symbols, characters and devices of representation is the outcome or effect, the cause of which is the artist's intuition of a particular form that determines the way in which a particular poem appeals to us. In other words, the material objects of a poem are given the power by the poets' intuition of its form to combine themselves and thus affect our ideas and emotions in a particular way. They might easily receive a different type of combination and might appeal to us differently had the form, which is the synthesizing principle, been of a different kind. Hence, the structural problem of a critic is to explain how the material aspects of a particular poem are related to its formal nature. This, however, by no way means that Crane suggests an investigation into the poet's mind to realize his intuition of form. He has warned us against such an assumption by suggesting time and again that the problem of the critic is not psychological but artistic. The poem as a concrete whole is there before the critic, and he must determine the formal nature of the poem from its material objects through hypotheses.

Hypothesis-making takes a very significant place in fact in Crane's method, and he considers it to be the first important step of the critic's work. The hypotheses, Crane suggests, must not be general but particular, concerned specially with the shaping principles of poetry. And in order to frame his hypotheses a critic must have some theoretical conception about the formal natures and material objects of poetry, although the fact remains that his previous conceptions of forms may be of on use for the poem in hand. Actually, the critic's theoretical knowledge will enable him to form some other hypotheses in the same manner. That is why Crane has suggested the necessity of theoretical analysis, in Aristotelian manner, of those literary genres which Aristotle could not do.

The hypotheses, again, must not merely be descriptive formulae. They must be formed in such a way that they clearly imply practical artistic consequences. Besides, a critic in his act of hypotheses-making must honour every aspect of the text as significant evidence. His hypothesis can never be accepted if it does not suit all the major and minor aspects of the poem. Crane has suggested a method of multiple hypotheses. His point is that the critic will at first frame all the possible hypotheses. In the next stage he will argue against each of them and thus try to dismiss each. In this way one hypothesis will remain, which cannot be dismissed. That will be the most appropriate hypothesis and will illustrate almost correctly the formal cause of the poem in question. A last point Crane mentions is that the critic must try to be as objective as possible at every step of his work.

Crane, however, is quite aware of the fact that all methods

have certain defects or, as he calls them, 'characteristic corruptions,' and, naturally, the formal approach to the structure of poetry which he speaks of is not free from its defects. Crane himself has mentioned three such possible faults which an incompetent practitioner of this method may indulge himself to make. Firstly, a critic may become merely formalistic in his concern with forms. He may then indulge more in the comparatively mechanical and dry job of analysing the various structural parts and the mechanism of how they combine than in pointing out what gives life to poetry. Secondly, in his concern with poetic wholes a critic may forget the importance of the words in poetry, which actually give a concrete body to a poem. And thirdly, a critic in this approach takes help of theoretical insights to solve the actual problems of structure. His purpose is not to propound or form any particular theory. But the critic may gradually fall into a 'methodological pedantry,' and may thus exhibit more interest in pronouncing the theoretical insights relevant to a problem than in the solution of that particular problem.

Crane's awareness of these defects of his own method shows his unbiased outlook as a theorist of poetry. He is among those few theorists who are squeamish about their own theories, and do not claim that theirs are the only faultless and correct methods.

However, in spite of its 'characteristic corruptions,' the theory of formal inquiry is more applicable to the problems of poetic structure than the contemporary modes of analysis for reasons more than one. Firstly, the faults of the formalistic approach to poetry are not part of the method. They are largely due to a lack of the critic's awareness of his actual work, or to some misconceptions on the critic's part. Naturally, a competent critic may easily avoid them and then give us adequate insights into the structural principles and characteristics of poetic works. Secondly, this method can do all the things which other contemporary modes of criticism usually perform. In an analysis of poetic structures the existing contemporary modes usually confine their investigation to the 'matter' (not 'form') of poetry and to the various techniques in which the matter is expressed in poetry. A critic who follows Crane's method of formal inquiry can and does perform such an investigation into the material elements of poetry. He may, for example, analyse how various elements in a poem are combined and how they work to create the desired effect; he may also explain the images, symbols, poetic diction and rhythm exploited in a poem, and may even tell us what an archetypal critic informs about the cultural and psychological universals that a poem implies. Thirdly, this approach can perform more than what other modes can, and herein lies the superiority of this mode. Unlike all other modes, the formalistic approach to poetic structure tries to find out the shaping principle of form that makes a poem an artistic whole of a particular kind. All other critical schools, Crane has rightly marked, have been in varying degrees generalizing and reductive. They approach a poem with some definite concepts about poetic structures and try to fit them to poems on the basis of some apparent analogies on the level of the material aspects of the poems. Thus, they reduce structures to a set of concepts.

Such positive values of Crane's theory may convince us of its relative greatness as well as of the liberal mindedness of the theorist. It may still appear to someone that Crane, even when he speaks repeatedly against dogmatism and reductionism, finally propounds his own theory in supersession of all other theories. L.C. Knights for example, in his review of Crane's *The Languages of Criticism and the Structure of Poetry* remarks: "[...] having discarded all terms derived from a world of discourse outside poetry Mr Crane seems to be left with a most meagre vocabulary of appraisal" (Knights "Review" 437). Such adverse criticism, however, can easily be disarmed and Crane's critical stand, which is popularly known as pluralism, may be understood if we follow what Crane has repeatedly said.

The first thing he says is that his theory is "only one of many possible legitimate approaches to the question of poetic structure" (Crane *Languages* 191). Thus, Crane unlike most other theorists, does not claim that his is the only fruitful and right method. The second important thing is that Crane's theory should not be misunderstood as one capable of solving all the critical problems. It is, Crane suggests, applicable only to the question of poetic structure and not to many other critical questions with which a critic may profitably concern himself. Crane believes that no single critical language can actually bring out the truth about literature. This belief is there as the basis of Crane's pluralism as well as of his disliking for dogmatism and reductionism. It is out of this belief, again, that he welcomes the existence of a multiplicity of critical languages, all of which together can make possible "a fuller exploration of our subject in its total extent than we could otherwise attain" (Crane *Languages* 193). It is clear, therefore, that to call Crane merely a formalistic critic or a neo-Aristotelian must be a great mistake. For a fuller understanding and exploration of literary texts he is ready to take help of any theory or approach he finds useful to solve his problem.

Crane believes, and quite rightly, that the hope for a glorious future of criticism depends on the perpetuation of this multiplicity as well as on an atmosphere of friendly cooperation among all the critical languages. For, the greatest bar to an advancement of criticism is not actually the existence of different schools of critics, but the spirit of exclusive dogmatism that keeps one school away from the other and prevents each one from taking help of others' insights. This problem of 'exclusive dogmatism' may be solved only if the critic possesses a self-knowledge. He should particularly know what he can perform—the limitations and positive values of what he does. He should try to know, with equal interest and sympathy, what other critics have achieved with their respective theories and methods. And above all he must try to bear in mind that the various critical languages are not "rival attempts to foreclose the 'real' or 'only profitable' truth about poetry," but are tools, "each with its peculiar capacities and limitations, for solving truly the many distinct kinds of problems which poetry, in its magnificent variety of aspects, presents to our view" (Crane *Languages* 194). We can hardly doubt that Crane's suggestions, if properly followed, will be of immense help to eradicate the unhealthy rivalry in the realm of critical languages, and to make criticism really fruitful and fairly comprehensive.

4

R.S. Crane and the Idea of the Humanities

Crane is a critical theorist and surely something more. We find him greatly interested in a "pursuit of a 'problematic' reconstruction of various modes of thought" (Crane *Humanities* Vol. I, xix). His observation on the problem of defining the humanities as well as his long critical survey of the changing concepts of the humanities from Vives to the present may prove it. Actually, controversies over the actual nature and function of the humanities are quite common at present. A large group of scholars and commoners think that a nation should, at the present stage of civilization, indulge more and more in the developments of higher technologies and practical sciences like electronics and computer engineering. It will, they believe, enable a nation to flourish and to protect itself from various destructive forces like war. Another group, on the contrary, nurtures the view that a proper training and study of the humanistic subject like history, literature, philosophy and languages may make us wise enough to avoid or fight out successfully any possible disaster. The problem attracts Crane and he turns his attention to the question of the meaning of the humanities as well as to the question of their place in western culture. His observations, as I shall exhibit, help to remove some popular misconceptions about the humanities and enable us to determine what should be the most appropriate attitude to them. Crane's theory of critical pluralism, or we may say his pluralistic temperament, also finds its expression in what he says about the humanities.

I

The question of what exactly the humanities are is a very difficult question indeed because even when all of us have some idea about them it becomes really problematic if we ask for an all inclusive and comprehensive definition of the humanities. Attempts have been made to define the humanities in two ways—either in terms of some subject matters or field of study, or in terms of the purposes or ends served by the humanities. Crane, however, finds faults with both the ways, and he suggests a third way which, he thinks, overcomes the limitations of the earlier definitions.

One of the traditional ways of defining the humanities is purely subject-oriented. In the universities and colleges we get the departments of humanities under which a number of subjects like languages and literature, fine arts, philosophy, history etc. are included. All these subjects are generally meant by the humanities, and those who remain engaged in teaching these subjects are taken to be humanists. Such a definition is, according to Crane, too simple and limited. It fails to point out the peculiar nature of the humanities. We hardly know why certain subjects are called the humanities. It cannot, again, properly distinguish the humanists from the non-humanists.

In the other way some authors of various ages have tried to define the humanities in terms of some purposes or ends supposed to be served by them. The assumption which acts behind this method is that certain human values are served more adequately by the so called humanistic subjects than either by the natural or by the social sciences. So the primary task is to determine the human values served by the humanities, and in this task authors are found to divide in two groups. In some writers the values are determined in terms of the intrinsic good of the soul, while in some others it is in terms of some external utility. The Spanish humanist Juan Luis Vives, for example, thinks that the humanities restore man to humanity and raise him toward God. John Stuart Mill's concept, on the contrary, is based chiefly on some external utility. He believes, that the humanities "prepare and discipline men for active life by inducing them to recognize that they are men before they are lawyers or physicians or merchants" (Crane *Humanities* Vol. I 6). However, after thus determining the ends of the humanities one can pronounce in the form of a definition that the humanities are those subjects in the study of which these already established ends are fulfilled.

The most obvious limitation of this way of defining the humanities is that ends are actually liable to differ as and when the modes of investigation differ. They depend on how we like to get them. And as our outlooks and requirements may quite naturally be different in different ages, the ends also change. Thus we never get a complete set of purposes served by the humanities, which means that our task of defining the humanities remains for ever incomplete. Another remarkable defect is that the various attempts to define the humanities in terms of the ends can offer us no means to achieve the ends. Crane also emphasizes this point when he says that the greatest weakness of these attempts is "their persistent vagueness about the means by which these ends are to be accomplished in the everyday affairs of education" (Crane *Humanities* Vol. I 6). Crane's point here is sound enough. Lofty ends will be of no help to us if we do not master the means to achieve them.

Crane, therefore, suggests a third way in which he tries to define the humanities in term neither of some specific subjects, nor of certain abstract purposes or ends of the humanities, but of some 'good arts' or principles. Crane identifies the humanities with the proper cultivation of certain arts or disciplines, which are actually means to some ends. The distinctive objects of the humanities are, Crane says, "what we commonly speak of as human achievements whether in sciences, in institutions, or in the arts" (Crane *Humanities* Vol. I 8). What Crane suggests is that the purely humanistic aspects of human achievements are the objects of the humanities and an understanding and appreciation of the unusual excellences of man is their distinctive aim. And in order to identify and understand those aspects in every field of human achievements we need a particular appropriate method of approach which is of utmost importance.

Crane, obviously, gives the greatest emphasis on the mode

of examination or method because he thinks that everything depends on the kinds of questions we ask. So a set of fixed techniques or arts must be there for the special purpose of exposing the humanistic aspects of human achievements. These arts or means however are not the humanities. They only lead us to understand the humanistic objects or we may say subjects, which are the ends. But in order to achieve the humanistic ends we must use no other method except the humanistic one. So Crane's impression, in short, is that the method or the technique, not the ends, is fixed, and the fixed humanistic method alone can ensure the ends. That's why Crane gives emphasis on the means and identifies the humanities with it.

However, we may now turn our attention to what, according to Crane, are the humanistic arts or means. Crane observes that most of the writers like philosophers, logicians, critics and historians from antiquity to the modern times have formulated different techniques which help to appreciate the humanistic aspects of human achievements. These techniques may roughly be classified into four principal groups of humanistic methods or arts, namely, linguistics, the analysis of ideas, literary and artistic criticism, and historiography, all of which collectively form the constituent elements of the humanities. These arts are supplementary to one another; each one of them points out certain different aspects. So the study of a subject will be complete only when we apply all of the arts applicable to that subject. A teacher of literature is thus required not merely to do a linguistic analysis of his text but also to point out the critical, philosophical and historical problems involved in it. In the language of Crane "the best teachers of language are those who, while being skilled in modern linguistic science, have also been trained to deal sensitively with the artistic and philosophical method; and the best teacher of history are those who know not merely how historical facts are derived but also how to deal competently with problems of ideas, of literary and artistic techniques and structures, and of symbolic expression" (Crane *Humanities* Vol. I 10).

In Crane's way of explanation the difference between the sciences and the humanities is the difference more of techniques and means than of subject matters. Even in the achievements of science humanistic aspects can be detected. But what is peculiarly or exclusively humanistic is the techniques or arts, the direction of which is almost the opposite of the direction taken by the scientific methods. Crane rightly observes that "the sciences are most successful when they seek to move from the diversity and particularity of their observations towards as high a degree of unity, uniformity, simplicity and necessity as their materials permit. The humanities, on the other hand, are most alive when they reverse this process, and look for devices of explanation and appreciation that will enable them to preserve as much as possible of the variety, the uniqueness, the unexpectedness, the complexity, the originality, that distinguish what men are capable of doing at their best from what they must do, or tend generally to do, as biological organisms or members of a community" (Crane *Humanities* Vol. I 12).

Crane thus makes it clear that the sciences and the humanities employ two completely different types of techniques or means and consequently arrive at completely different types of ends. Thus there remains no rivalry between these two streams of knowledge. This explanation will surely help to remove the popular misconception that the humanities now-a-days have been threatened by the rapid development of the natural and social sciences. Real threats, Crane has rightly observed, come to the humanities from within, not from without. They are the spirits of dogmatism and reductionism—those twin monsters which oppose and often make impossible a proper cultivation of the humanistic arts. Dogmatism gives birth to various rival schools of critics, linguists, philosophers and historians, each one of which is engaged to a great extent in finding faults with others, neglecting what they can contribute to the totality of thought. It spoils the scope of employing all the available resources of analysis and appreciation. Again, there remains a sense of jealousy among the experts of the different humanistic arts, each one of whom claims his own art to be of supreme importance, forgetting the fact that all the arts are supplementary to one another. Thus, dogmatism hampers to a pernicious degree a proper study and training in all the 'good arts.' The other enemy to the humanities is reductionism which is not less harmful than dogmatism. The spirit of reductionism keeps our attention away from the diversity of human achievements and thus denies the essential spirit of the humanities, which lies in diversity.

In Crane's idea of the humanities, however, no subversive spirit like dogmatism and reductionism is allowed. Crane claims that his idea of the humanities, if properly cultivated, will fight these spirits out. There is of course sense in what he says. For, his idea demands a proper cultivation of all the four arts and a good relation among them. Another point to note here is that the way in which Crane solves the problem of defining the humanities is quite compatible with the whole critical thought of Crane. His theory of critical pluralism is meant to remove the unhealthy and meaninglless rivalry and jealousy among the various critical schools and also to cause a situation of mutual help. The desirable function of the humanistic arts as Crane has expressed is quite in tune with this spirit.

II

After defining the humanities in a different way Crane has engaged himself in some sort of a historical survey of how scholars of different ages have defined and evaluated the humanities in some distinctive ways. He starts his observation with Vives. However, Crane believes that it is Quintilian, not Vives, who long ago initiated a particular approach to the humanities which later scholars inherited.

As a teacher and practising advocate Quintilian was equally interested in rhetoric and perfection of man. In *The Training of an Auditor,* a book which is divided into twelve parts, he considers rhetoric broadly under three heads: art, the artist, and the work. In the course of doing this he brings all these three aspects into a significant relationship of interdependence. Quintilian's modernity mainly lies in his reaction against the contemporary decadence in style and taste. A serious champion of education he enumerated the defects of the existing system in all its stages, and emphasized the need for common sense and an imitation of nature. He based his theory on nature, reason and experience. He definitely states that his intention is not to put forward rules that are universally and invariably applicable, but rather to inculcate general principles suggestive of the main truths. (Here Quintilian has distinct affinity with the stand of Crane who also believes that no universal formula can describe literary qualities.) Quintilian held that Art, far from being in conflict with nature, is, in fact, based on observation of nature's ways. He, therefore, endorses the familiar doctrine of the need for natural capacity which should be activated by art and improved by practice. Nature, art and practice are the three requisites for perfection. Although Quintilian believed in the primacy of speech he held at the same time that everyday speech in itself is inadequate, that it is required to be raised to a higher power for artistic purposes, and he devotes a long time in suggesting how words can be combined in different ways for effective communication. He divides the figures into figures of speech and figures of thought, a distinction which is often lost sight of by rhetoricians. In regard to style Quintilian's recommendation was that one must go for the choice of the best words and their most effective arrangement involving an exploitation of all the resources of language. In this respect Quintilian anticipates Coleridge's recommendation for "the best words in the best order" (Hazlitt *Table Talk VI* 293). Briefly, as the last great exponent of classicism at Rome Quintilian put forward a creed that differed in some important aspects from those of his predecessors, though animated by the same principles of order, design and fitness, and making for the same goal of clarity of thought and expression.

In terms of the humanities Quintilian's stand is very clear. Clarity of thought and clarity of expression alone can make a man a good unit in the society. A training in rhetoric and a concern with the potentialities of the language would make one able to see things in broader perspective and would induce him to cultivate a broad, liberal or humanistic attitude towards life.

According to the Romans what made man different from animal was speech. Perfection of speech, therefore, leads to the perfection of man. This happens in a number of ways. At the personal level the effort to articulate one's thoughts makes one conscious of his inabilities and the tyranny of the language. At the social level speech is the means of communication and makes man a social being. Although Quintilian flourished in the first century A.D. Christianity had not yet made a dent in the Roman civilization. So Quintilian's argument can be treated as pagan, or at least falling outside the purview of Christianity. Right from the Renaissance Christianity begins to pervade the texture of European civilization so that gradually it became impossible to think of the total man or the fullest man without taking into consideration his religious aspect. The Humanism of Irving Babbitt was contested by Eliot on the ground of religion. Eliot held that "the humanistic point of view is auxiliary to and dependent upon the religious point of view" (Eliot *Selected Essays* 480).

Crane picks up Vives as "an early modern Quintilian," because of the affinity between Quintilian and Vives in regard to their definitions and evaluations of the humanities. But the important point that Crane tries to make us see is that Vives surpasses Quintilian on account of his emphasis on religion. Vives says: "What can we fix as the end of man, except God Himself?" (Crane *Humanities* Vol. I 32). For Vives the Christian God is the God of love, and it is the cultivation of love in its Christian sense of selfless dedication and devotion that can improve the relation between individuals as well as the relation between the individual and the society.

At this point of his observation Crane shows an unexpected affinity with Eliot regarding the role of religion in the life of a man and the society. Without religious awareness man remains incomplete. Unless one is awakened by love which illuminates life man can never realize the full value of the humanities. The affinity becomes reinforced when Crane refers to the *Divine Comedy* "as an expression of man achieving selfhood through absorption into the Mind of God" (Crane *Humanities* Vol. I 39). Eliot also writes: "The experience of a poem is the experience both of a moment and of a lifetime. It is very much like our intenser experiences of other human beings [...]. Dante's is one of those which one can only just hope to grow up to at the end of life" (Eliot *Selected Essay* 250-51). He also says that the "enjoyment of the *Divine Comedy* is a continuous process" (Eliot *Selected Essay* 238). Again, as Crane compares Dante with Shakespeare, similarly Eliot also compares Shakespeare and Dante in his essay on Dante. Crane seems to agree with Vives, and later with Eliot, that the fullest realization of man is not possible without religious awareness. This new dimension of the humanities is, according to Crane, the most significant contribution of Vives, who otherwise has most things common with his great Roman predecessor Quintilian.

The five 16th century humanists—Erasmus, Montaigne, Elyot, Ascham and Sidney—are found to form, in a broad sense, a homogeneous group because of the fact that they all employ, in order to formulate their problems, the same distinction of words and things. And by virtue of the basic distinction employed by them they may be said to continue the tradition of Quintilian and Vives. However, solutions to the problems of education or culture are often seen to vary as either words or things are emphasized. In Quintilian the primacy of speech (words) is asserted, whereas in Vives it is 'reason' or 'practical wisdom' (things) that gets prominence. The 16th century humanists also give prominence to matter. But at the same time they believe in the interrelation of expression and content. They are conscious of the fact that the primary way to acquire a knowledge of the matter is through words, because the source to which one goes for matter is books, and books express their matters through words. The chief aim of education for all of them is effective guidance of human actions. And this aim can best be achieved by the study of those authors who have in their writings dealt with human virtues and actions in eloquent languages. Thus almost all of these humanists prescribe the reading of classical texts.

However, this does not mean that the 16th century humanists were unanimous in all the issues. Crane has considered them individually, showing where they differ from one another as well as their individual contributions. In Erasmus, for example, Crane finds a unity of both literary and biblical criticism. Erasmus's ends are both moral and religious. It is, Crane observes, "a kind of humanism which seeks its values in the study of documents and writers rather than in the systematic consideration of doctrine" (Crane *Humanities* Vol. I 45). This tradition in humanism, Crane also observes, comes to the moderns through such eminent critics as Matthew Arnold and T.S. Eliot. Eliot's essay on Dante may be considered as an excellent example in hand. Crane thus links Erasmus to one of the greatest poet-critics of our century.

Ascham and Sidney also, like Erasmus, talk of human actions and virtues chiefly in terms of an interpretation and evaluation of words. Their ultimate aim is of course to expose the essential matter or impart wisdom which we require to achieve perfection in actions. But they like to do so through grammatical and critical investigation of words. But the two other humanists of the 16th century, Sir Thomas Elyot and Montaigne, concentrate their attention primarily on things rather than on words. Crane observes that "they (Elyot and Montaigne) also treat of languages, authors, and arts, but their primary problem is the statement of principles or precepts relevant directly to the characters and behaviour of men in active life" (Crane *Humanities* Vol. I 45).

Elyot is concerned chiefly with the education of those who take part in the important activities of the state, whereas Montaigne concerns himself not with the character of the civil servants or men engaged in important works of the state, but with that of "the private gentleman living a life of worldly but cultured ease on his estate, conversing with his friends, reading books, and above all [...] seasoning his understanding with a philosophy which will teach him to know himself and how both well to die and well to live" (Crane *Humanities* Vol. I 45). Education, for Montaigne, should aim at giving general human wisdom, rather than technical specialization. It is, according to Montaigne, nothing but pedantry to spend much time in teaching grammar, rhetoric, or the art of forming syllogisms when, in practical life, we require to know natural and simple manner of speaking, which is the best of all. Students should be exposed to different languages at a very early age so that they may pick them up. Foreign travels and conversations with men are equally important.

Crane thus considers the 16th century humanists and points

out the modifications which humanism underwent in the hands of its 16th century practitioners. Montaigne's emphasis on the natural way of speaking as well as on the generalized aim of education is one of them. And in this emphasis we may trace the origin of the concept of natural education—the concept which received some popularity in the 18th century in the great French philosopher Rousseau.

However, the 17th century is also not less significant in the history of the humanities. It is in the 17th century, Crane observes, that the long tradition of the humanities, as the study of good ancient literature was opposed by the newer tradition of natural science. Crane has called it a conflict between letters and natural philosophy. Side by side another type of conflict also emerged in this century. This other conflict, Crane observes, was the conflict between ancient and modern literature and learning. Both the conflicts had long-term effects on the conceptions and discussions of the humanities in the later ages.

The chief exponents of the first type of conflict, however, were Bacon and Descartes. The Renaissance humanists, unlike Bacon and Descartes, evaluated the classics and the various other arts in the context of a 'philosophy,' oriented to the guidance of human actions. Natural sciences or the discovery of truths about things were not so seriously considered in that philosophy. They were only viewed as means to some non-scientific ends. In short, the 'philosophy' of the Renaissance humanists had its basis on some other arts like history, poetry, oratory and the precepts of the moral philosophers. But in the philosophies of Bacon and Descartes, Crane observes, the natural sciences do not remain insignificant, or merely as a means to some non-scientific ends. In their philosophies inquiries into natural phenomena are raised to a "position in which they become, in one way or another, basic to all the rest of learning" (Crane *Humanities* Vol. I 56). Both Bacon and Descartes, Crane has observed through illustrations of their works, have advocated the supremacy of the study of natural philosophy over linguistic and literary studies. And they exerted a tremendous influence on a large number of their followers, who proposed various reformations of the system of education as well as of the subjects to be studied. They emphasized the discovery of the true nature of things instead of the past tradition of linguistic and literary studies. Sir William Petty in his short pamphlet "Advice [...] to Mr. Hartlib for the Advancement of Some Particular Parts of Learning," John Hall in *An Humble Motion*, and Abraham Cowley in his *Proposition for the Advancement of Experimental Philosophy* have given different projects for the reformation of schools and universities because these educational institutions, according to their opinion, confine themselves to linguistic studies and to some unintelligible verbalisms of scholastic philosophy and thus neglect the studies which can give substantive knowledge. They, however, do not intend to banish logic and rhetoric altogether, but they clearly express it in their projects of reformation that primary emphasis must be given on the study of natural philosophy, mechanical experiments, chemistry, a scientific study of history and such other subjects that may give real knowledge of things. Thus, Crane observes, the 17th century initiates a new debate in the field of humanism—the debate that continues to exist in varying forms in all the later periods and thus occupies an important place in any consideration of the evolution of the humanities.

The century is also remarkable in the history of the humanities for an initiation of the conflict between the ancient and modern literature and learning. Some of the 17th century humanists like George Hakewill, Joseph Glanvill and Charles Perrault make a distinction between the old and the modern and believe in the superiority of the latter. They compare the achievements of the moderns and the ancients in the different fields of knowledge and then assert the idea of progress from antiquity to the modern times. They explain this progress as a part of the necessary law of human development. The two basic assumptions upon which their arguments rest are, firstly, that human powers (both intelligence and basic capacities) have remained more or less the same throughout ages, and, secondly, that the development of knowledge and the arts depends largely on experience as well as the inventions and application of the correct method of reasoning. And the matter of experience and invention of the correct method is subject to the passage of time. Naturally, the moderns are likely to offer us more than the ancients because they possess a comparatively matured form of experience.

Sir William Temple, however, is among those others who emerge as extreme defenders of the ancients. Temple tries to refute the assumptions upon which Perrault and others developed their idea of the relative progress of the moderns. His arguments are not very convincing. But the important point here is not so much how convincingly one refutes other's arguments as the fact that the quarrel is there among the 17th century writers over the issue. And in order to exhibit the influence of this quarrel Crane has mentioned two books—one of the 16th century and the other of the 18th—which point out the wide difference between the two writers with regard to their ideas. In Vives's *The Transmission of Disciplines* we do not corne across any historical distinction of earlier and later, or ancient and modern. In other words, the tradition of the humanities for Vives was a single tradition in which there was no time bound division of old and new. But Hugh Blair, the 18th century humanist, considers in his book *Lectures on Rhetoric and Belles Letters* the problem of time to be an important factor in the inclusion of authors in an educational programme. He thinks it proper to study the comparative merits of the ancients and the moderns.

It may passingly be noted here that long before Blair's book was published (1783), the comparative merits and demerits of the ancients and the moderns were already a matter of great debate in England. This debate, in fact, formed an important part of the 17th century critical climate. Dryden's book *An Essay of Dramatic Poesy*, published in 1668, succinctly sums up this important critical issue in the debate between Crites and Eugenius. In course of this debate Crites argues that poetry was held in greater esteem by the ancients, and the ancients were more faithful imitators of nature. Even earlier, Ben Jonson had admitted their (of the ancients) superiority, and he imitated and borrowed from them. But Eugenius replies that the moderns should not follow the ancients, but nature which was also imitated by the ancients. Furthermore, Eugenius argues—an argument that has persisted till our time—that we are taller than our ancestors because we stand on their shoulders. In other words, the moderns have the advantage of deriving the benefit of the wisdom of the ancients, while the ancients, for obvious historical reasons, are denied the wisdom of the modern.

The discussion of Crites and Eugenius is of considerable interest in the history of literary criticism, as it was this issue that led to the division of the French Academy and became a matter of almost European controversy. The quarrel of the ancients and the modern began in Italy where it arose out of a debate on the relative supremacy of Tasso and Ariosto. It was introduced into France about 1635 by Boisrobert.

What is important to note is Crane's conspicuous omission of Dryden who has dealt with the relative merits by 1668 and, not in any spirit of partisanship though, he sympathises with the moderns; and some of the arguments which he adduced, on one side or the other, wait to be used in the great quarrel between Perrault and Boileau. In this respect Dryden should be considered as the leader of the modern school in England through whose writings the debate was introduced to England and on account of whose fine critical insight to see the issue in broad perspective, the debate took a very definite shape, and influenced the subsequent course of literary criticism.

However, the quarrel of the moderns and the ancients, Crane observes, had a great impact on the humanities. The first important thing is that the quarrel broadens the scope of the humanities to include the modern poets, historians, philosophers and others into the educational programmes. Another important effect of the quarrel is that the various discussions on the issue become important to the later history of the humanities in two different ways. In the first place, as Crane says, "it is largely to these numerous discussions of ages of learning in the 17th century that we must trace the increasing vogue, since then, of cultural history as a kind of general framework of more or less sharply differentiated periods each with its peculiar characteristics or conditions, within which human achievements in the arts and science must be placed if they are to be properly explained and evaluated" (Crane *Humanities* Vol. I 86-87). This observation of Crane is highly original in the sense that it marks the beginning of our general awareness of the cultural history, which is now closely related to any remarkable approach to poetry, history, or philosophy. In the second place "the particular schematism of ages of culture which emerged from the discussions of the seventeenth century is still, for the most part, the schematism employed, often with the same relative evaluations of ages, in popular histories of science or civilization and in most university courses on the humanities" (Crane *Humanities* Vol. I 87).

In the 18th century Crane marks a different approach to the humanities. The attention was shifted from the problems of the nature of things to the questions related to the human nature or the humanities themselves. Naturally, the opposition between scholastic philosophy and the humanities, which was in vogue in the Renaissance, or the 17th century opposition between the humanities and natural science takes a different direction in this century. It is of course true that a contrast between literature and philosophy still exists. But it is not actually in the form of an opposition between the principles of philosophy and those of the humanities. Philosophy is treated as complementary to the humanities in the sense that the humanists endeavour to deal philosophically with the humanistic subject matters of language, rhetoric, criticism and history. Thus the 18th century writers, making philosophy as the basis of all sorts of knowledge, attempted to achieve some sort of a harmony or balance among the various rival interests of the earlier periods. Crane has illustrated what Edward Gibbon says in his book *Essai sur l'etude de la literature* as an example of the typical 18th century approach to the humanities—an "approach which emphasises particulars and distrusts systems and yet seeks a philosophic basis for its operations" (Crane *Humanities* Vol. I 93).

The new philosophy which is there at the centre of all humanistic discussions of the 18th century may be called a philosophy of the human mind because it takes as its primary subject matter the mind of man, not the objects of nature. Some of the great writers of the period like John Locke, David Hume, Thomas Reid and Dugald Stewart, who are the proponents of this new philosophy, believed that there must be some natural order or system in all the functionings of the human mind, on the basis of which they aspired to construct the science of human nature. What they were required to do for a philosophy of the mind was to systematize the various operations of the mind under some generalised principles in the form of certain universal laws. Such a systematization of the multifarious operations of the mind, Hume suggests, will enable the philosophers to represent the various activities and progress of man as related ones.

Crane has mentioned George Campbell's *The Philosophy of Rhetoric* as an illustration of how the 18th century writers sought to give the new philosophical orientation to the humanistic subject of rhetoric. Campbell's purpose in this book, Crane observes, was "not to restate or rearrange the classical rules but rather to relate the particular effects of rhetorical composition to their cause in the faculties and operations of the mind—in short, to make rhetoric 'philosophical' by showing its connections with the science of human nature" (Crane *Humanities* Vol. I 97). Campbell achieves his aim by dividing the faculties of the mind under four heads and then connecting each of the humanistic arts of history, poetry (both narrative and dramatic) and rhetoric to each of the faculties.

In a way Campbell anticipates some of the findings of I.A. Richards who in his *Principles of Literary Criticism* (first published in 1924) said that a theory of criticism must take into account the communication, and argued that "sensation, imagery, feeling, emotion, together with pleasure, unpleasure and pain are names for the conscious characteristics of impulses" (Richards 92). In fact, through the analysis of a poem in *Principles of Literary Criticism* he shows with the help of a diagram how this happens.

However, regarding criticism or the art of poetry Crane observes that the 18th century idea of criticism was closely connected to rhetoric. Of course there were criticisms of poetry and poets which were not directly related to or dependent on rhetoric. Still "the ends if poetry are frequently given as identical with the rhetorical ends of pleasing, instructing, and moving; the treatment of style is usually the same in the two contexts"

(Crane *Humanities* Vol. I 99). Besides, the 18th century humanistic writers tended to give a philosophical basis to criticism by using principles mostly derived from the natural faculties and operations of the mind.

In order to give us an idea of the 18th century discussions on the art of history Crane refers to Bolingbroke's *Letters on the Study and Use of History.* For Bolingbroke, Crane observes, "The true use of history is to make us not more learned but better men and better citizens" (Crane *Humanities* Vol. I 100). In Bolingbroke's definition history is philosophy teaching by examples. The examples of history, Bolingbroke suggests, have some general and remote influence on our minds. They, thus, help us to form some sort of a philosophic sense, which may lead us to rise from the particular examples of history to general knowledge and guide our conducts in all the situations of private and public life.

One important thing Crane has missed here is that Bolingbroke was not the first to suggest that history was a kind of philosophy teaching by examples. About 150 years before the publication of Bolingbroke's *Letters on the Study and Use of History,* Sir Philip Sidney in his *An Apologie For Poetrie,* while comparing poetry with philosophy and history, remarked: "At length, the long lyne of theyr disputation maketh a poynt in thys, that the one giveth the precept and the other the example" (Sidney 15). Sidney was more acute and realistic than Bolingbroke when he pointed out, though in a different context, that the example provided by history is tied down to facts. He writes: "the historian [...] is so tyed, not to what shoulde bee, but to what is; to the particular truth of things and not to the general reason of things; that hys example draweth no necessary consequence, and therefore a lesse fruitfull doctrine" (Sidney 17).

However, from the various discussions about the humanistic arts in the 18th century Crane endeavours to point out the nature of the humanistic studies during that period. He observes that the essential nature of the humanistic study in the 18th century is similar in many respects to that of the Renaissance. The emphasis is still there on grammar, rhetoric, poetry, history and philosophy. Crane, however, does not mean to suggest that the 18th century discussions on the humanities should be regarded as a simple continuation of the Renaissance humanism. The 16th century humanists were mainly concerned with how the different disciplines of the humanistic arts might be effectively utilised as guides to the actions of man as an individual as well as a member of the society. This problem still persists in the 18th century, but not as the most prominent one. The centre of interest, instead, in almost all the discussions of the century is "a problem of method in the humanities themselves—the problem, specifically, of how, in disciplines that have to do essentially with the judgment of writers, writings, and facts, the particularity of the material can be illuminated in its treatment or in its uses by the spirit of reason or philosophic generality" (Crane *Humanities* Vol. I 102). A last point Crane mentions is that in the 18th century an attempt was there to achieve some kind of organic unification of the various particular humanistic arts.

If the 18th century in the history of the humanities can be considered as an age of harmony or balance among the various rival interests of the earlier periods, in the 19th century the history of the humanities once again becomes a history of rivalry and opposition. It was a period of attack and defence so far as the humanities were concerned.

The various attacks on the humanities in this century, Crane observes, came mainly from two different groups of intellectuals—one is the group of the Utilitarians or Philosophical Radicals, and the other is that of the propagandists for physical science. Jeremy Bentham and James Mill were the leaders of the first group, who undertook, as their main problem, the task of educating the rising generation. They formulated the general principles of education in utilitarian terms, and their utilitarian stand goes against literature or even the humanities in general. In Mill's formulation of educational principles, however, the hostility to the humanities is only suggested. But some of Mill's followers like Thomas Southwood Smith were direct in their attack on the humanities. Smith, for instance, finds that the classical languages and literature are of no use for those who, in future, are destined to devote themselves to the ordinary business of life. Smith not merely condemns the linguistic and literary studies as useless, but considers them as "harmful survivals from medieval times" (Crane *Humanities* Vol. I 129). Modern world, he maintains, is a world chiefly of science and mechanical art. Naturally, the dominance of the humanistic subjects in the curricula of schools and colleges is inimical to progress.

The other group of intellectuals who may be regarded as the propagandists for physical science has also established the comparative greatness of science. Thomas Henry Huxley, for example, argues that the 19th century world is remarkably different from the Renaissance or the medieval world. There was then no remarkable development of physical science. Naturally the effort of the humanists for making the humanistic subjects the foundation of education was of great service to mankind. But now a man needs the knowledge of physical science more than that of the humanities. What Huxley, therefore, tries to do in a number of essays is to make science, rather than the humanities, the foundation of education.

However, the 19th century humanists, Crane observes, forcefully reacted against this attack, and met the challenge of the friends of science. He also observes that the humanists followed two different ways to defend themselves against their opponents. In the first place a group of specialists in some humanistic arts attempted to "model their disciplines on canons of inquiry in the natural science" (Crane *Humanities* Vol. I 138). They endeavoured to give a scientific orientation to the humanities by applying scientific methods to them, and thus make them conform to the scientific spirit of the age. In the second place another group of humanist educators concerned themselves with the principles as well as contents of education and this shows that the humanistic subjects are as important to study, if not more, as the scientific subjects. They tried to reassert the universal and permanent value of letters and philosophy.

Crane has organized the opinions and discussions of different humanistic writers to expose the real nature of the defence of the humanities in the 19th century. He has effectively analysed how various eminent writers of the period have tried to give a scientific basis to the study of the humanistic subjects of language, literary analysis and history. Side by side Crane has analysed the observations of William Whewell, Cardinal Newman, John Stuart Mill, and Matthew Arnold, and has exhibited how these intellectuals and educationists, in order to defend the humanities, have formulated some new principles of education which express the specific values of humanities, distinguished from the values of science. Thus, in the manner of an impartial observer and faithful historian Crane records what actually happened in the field of the humanities during this century.

It is more or less clear from Crane's observation that the values or ends of the humanities were not supposed to be the same in all the ages. Even the very concept of the humanities is not uniform. Sometimes they are equated with certain subject-matters, and at some other times they are conceived as a set of arts or principles. The ends of the humanities are also modified or changed by writers of different ages according to the nature of their problems. Vives, for example, considers the humanities as a means to restore man to humanity and to raise him to God. For Sidney the humanistic arts give us a knowledge of ourselves, which does not end in well-knowing but leads us to well-doing. Sir Thomas Elyot thinks that the humanistic arts can prepare a man better than anything else to be a prudent, just and temperate magistrate. Milton also believes that the peculiar values of the humanities must be determined in terms of the important task they perform to make a man fit for all the occasions of his private and public life.

However, in spite of all such differences with regard to the particular ends the humanistic arts are believed to serve, there is, Crane observes, a basic unity among all the humanistic writers. He also finds that this unity lies with the fact that they inherit the essential terms and manners of their discussions about the humanities from the Roman scholars Cicero and Quintilian. Even the 20th century humanists are not an exception to this, because, as Crane observes, "the humanities [...] have been in the modern period, no less than for the Romans, means to the realization of some ideal or use over and above the understanding and appreciation of the peculiarly human achievements in art or philosophy or science which have been their subject matter" (Crane *Humanities* Vol. I 158).

In the twentieth century, Crane observes, we have inherited the 19th century quarrel between the humanities and natural science. The quarrel has rather taken a more acute form with the growing popularity of the social science in the present century. The humanities at present have thus faced a double enemy. Crane is surely right to conclude that a rapid and popular growth of the various vocational subjects and their inclusion in the school curricula have increased a general neglect of the classical languages at present. These vocational subjects are found to yield quicker result in establishing a man in his practical life. A study of the classical languages can hardly be found so useful to a man in his practical life as these professional subjects.

However, Crane divides the 20th century humanists into two groups. In the first group he includes those scholars who are known as philologists, textual critics, bibliographers, biographers, and literary historians. Their chief concern is with the factual arts or techniques of literary study. They deal primarily with the external aspects of literature and give us facts. The other group of humanists—the critics—on the contrary, are mainly concerned with the appreciation and understanding of the literary works. They (the critics) seek to "maintain the normative character of literary study and its concern with literary substance in opposition to the scientific preoccupations of the scholars" (Crane *Humanities* Vol. I 165). The critics, Crane finds, have done this in two major ways. In one way the problems of literary criticism have been taken primarily as problems of expression. And the critics who follow this way believe that the problems of criticism can best be solved in terms of the semantic analysis of literary texts. Critics like I.A. Richards, J.C. Ransom, and Kenneth Burke who may and do widely differ in all other respects are found to unite at this point. In another way the major problem of criticism is the problem of relating the poems or other literary works to experience or to the broader aspects of life. The critics belonging to the Marxist and psychological schools of criticism, for example, tend to do this very thing.

Crane thus observes that the literary scholars (including the textual critics, biographers, bibliographers and philologists) are there on the one hand, and the literary critics on the other forming two dominant schools of literary humanists in our century. And "the striking thing about them is that they represent, though with a more modern accent, the same twofold constitution of the arts of humanistic study—grammar and historical exegesis on the one hand and rhetoric on the other—which we saw first in Quintilian and then in the Renaissance and which, in the eighteenth century, appeared in the quarrels of Bentley and Pope" (Crane *Humanities* Vol. I 166). Crane thus connects the 20th century humanism to the long tradition of humanistic studies in the past. What is perhaps more important is that Crane finds the origins of modern scholarly and critical investigations in the grammatical-historical and rhetorical studies of the past centuries.

It may, however, be said that there is nothing very original about Crane so far as his essays on the humanities are concerned. He organizes and illustrates how the concept of the humanities have changed as well as how they have been treated from period to period. One may also feel that Crane should have included Sidney and given due importance to Dryden which, as I have exhibited, he so strongly deserves. But Crane may be defended on the ground that it is an excusable omission in a work where the whole issue is seen in the light of the development of the humanities and their 'shifting definitions and evaluations.' And what is above everything else is that a historical study of the changing concepts of the humanities from the Renaissance, which Crane has so successfully done, will surely help us to understand the nature of the humanities at present as well as in the coming ages. Such a history, we must agree with Crane, enables us "first of all, to appreciate better the significance of what is being said and done with respect to the humanities in education at the present time and, more important still, to make possible a more adequate answer [...] to the general questions on which our inquiry has turned, namely: what is the nature of the humanities? And what in view of their history and their present state, is the direction in which we should wish them to go in the future" (Crane *Humanities* Vol. I 155).

5

Critical and Historical Principles of Literary History: Crane's Stand

Crane has investigated in detail the basic characters of different types of literary histories, the elements required to construct them, their limitations, and has suggested in the light of his investigations the primary requirements and method of writing the most effective and fruitful literary history. He is perhaps the first to investigate systematically the techniques of writing literary history. One can come across scattered remarks in the writings of other critics and literary historians, but there is hardly any such detailed and comprehensive study of the historical and critical aspects of literary history. Crane may, therefore, claim the credit of exploring an yet unexplored region.

Literary history, Crane observes, comprises two main elements—one historical and the other critical. The first one includes terms which signify actions, characters, habits, aims and circumstances of writers. All these actually help the historian to construct the continuous narrative which is a 'must' for any type of history. History is not a collection of disconnected or separated incidents or events but a continuous narrative of some sort of development. The various parts or units of this continuum must be organically connected. The other element of a literary history is the critical analysis of literary texts—the properties of their language, aesthetic problems, structural hazards of the artists and also the impact of the works on readers. The historian's training and industry in historical research, and his intelligence and sensitivity to literary history depends on the quality of the historical sensibility of the scholar writing the history. And as differences are quite common in such matters, various types of literary histories emerge. The historian's sensitivity to certain work is, again, guided by his attachment to any of the various critical schools, and the character of his critical findings is dependent on the critical outlook of the particular school to which he belongs.

With regard to the critical propositions for their literary histories almost all the literary historians are generally seen to follow two modes of critical inquiry. One is the philological method in which the "essential instruments are textual and historical criticism, grammar (including prosody), the grammatical parts of logic, and bibliography in the traditional sense" (Crane *Literary History* 3). This method is certainly helpful, though not faultless, because a historian can, with the help of these instruments and his knowledge of human affairs, make precise and verifiable statements about literary texts. Another method of critical inquiry is called 'dialectical method,' the primary reference in which is different from that of the philological method. While the primary reference in the philological method is to the historical origin of works, in the dialectical method it is to their effects upon readers. Crane however does not suspect the legitimacy of these critical modes in the writing of literary history. But his objection is due to the fact that they are not free from limitations. Neither of them can consider literary works as artistic wholes. The sense of the wholeness of a literary work, with which the philological critic is concerned is nothing but the grammatical completeness of the text. His problems are mainly related to parts, the solutions of which are independent of inferences from the whole. And the wholes in the other mode are only "dialectical compositions of qualities inhering the author as unifying source, with the result that what he (the critic) is able to discriminate in works are, again, only the characteristics of parts" (Crane *Literary History* 11). Crane's objection to the philological mode of criticism is chiefly because it can investigate only the preconstructional aspects—the aspects of origin and source of a work—and he reacts against the dialectical method because its concern is mainly with the post-constructional aspects (that is, the effects of completed works on readers). But the constructional aspects, the aspects of artistic principles and judgments engaged in the act of actual composition, are not adequately treated. Even in relation to the preconstructional and the post-constructional aspects they frame only some general statements which can hardly establish the distinguishing characters of individual literary works.

Therefore, Crane offers a third mode of critical investigation which he calls 'the concept of artistic synthesis' and which, he claims, will be free from the limitations of the other two methods. Every literary creation in this mode is accepted to be an individual whole. Crane's point is that literary works, artistically considered, are different from one another in two respects—in respect of the wholeness achieved by the artist and in respect of his handling of the parts for their proper synthesizing. And the critical speculations of a historian can never be complete unless he takes into account both these aspects. Crane's method is basically different from others in respect of the *artistic* ends it finally seeks to achieve. In the philological analysis the ends are only historically known intentions of the writers, and in the dialectical analysis they are ideal ends, deduced from comparative study of different types of arts or activities. But in Crane's method of critical analysis there remains no idea of an ideal form of poetry or drama or novel because the critic here is not primarily concerned with comparison. "His (the critic's) first business, whatever else he may do, is to consider literary works, without prejudice, in the light of the specific ends or principles of construction, whatever they may be, which have in fact, on the best hypothesis he can form, governed their composition and of the theoretically known conditions of maximum excellence peculiar to each" (Crane *Literary History* 16). Crane's point here is understandable. He means to suggest that even within the same genre the principles of construction may and do vary from work to work. Each one is a unique production of art, different from others in appeal and impact. So there can be no ideal form of literature, and instead of judging one work in the light of another, it is better and more fruitful to examine the peculiar principles and ends relating to the production of that work.

What Crane claims here may theoretically be justified by saying that the artistic and structural properties of literary works may fruitfully be analysed without any comparative study among them. It can also be admitted that the concept of an 'ideal form' may be a bar to such analysis. The difference in fact is the difference between examining whether a literary work is 'good' or 'great.' Goodness of a literary work can be examined by literary criteria alone. A close structural analysis can establish whether it is a good poem. But if we are to consider whether the poem under consideration is also a great poem we have to step beyond the immediate frame of reference and place the poem by the side of other great poems and evaluate it. Two tools of criticism must be in operation: analysis and comparison. Analysis is necessary for bringing out the intrinsic qualities of a poem or any literary work for that matter within the framework of the work itself. But comparison is inevitable if we want to determine the place of a literary work in literary history. History thus cannot completely avoid value judgment. A literary history is not just a record of literary events; it is a discourse on continuous literary movements in which every literary work makes some contribution howsoever significant or insignificant it may be. But the historian is obliged to assess the nature of that significance in terms of literary history. The problem with the generic approach, on the other hand, is that the critic often has a tendency to move beyond the immediate literary work on hand and dilate on its relation to the genre to which it belongs. It is true that in order to examine *Macbeth* as a tragedy one has to consider the notions of an ideal tragedy and how the Shakespearean play conforms to or departs from these notions. Besides, we can hardly remove ideas from our minds even if we try to do so. In course of reading and examining various literary texts, the tendency may easily grow to form, through conscious or unconscious comparisons of various literary works, an idea of the best type of poetry or drama or novel. We at least become conscious of what type of works interests us more. Crane's preference for the method of structural analysis for a literary historian becomes more or less the same as the New Critic's claim of objectivity in literary criticism. Both are almost impossible in the practical field simply because human mind is far from being a machine. In this realistic approach to the human predicament involved in literary criticism Crane reinforces what Eliot said in 1930: "To suppose that anyone likes only the *best* poetry, and that he likes all the best poetry equally, and that he likes all the second best poetry in a second best liking and so on until he detests all of the worst poetry equally is to suppose a monster" (Eliot "Propaganda" 595-602).

Crane also admits that the type of critical analysis which he suggests is not very simple, and that there is great chance of being misled and of achieving a wrong judgment. The critic may be a victim of 'formalism'—the tendency to reduce the problems of artistic form to questions of structure merely. Another possible error is that the critic may confuse artistic principles with techniques.

These two possible errors however, Crane suggests, may be avoided with the help of two things. One is the historian's experience. He must be widely and critically read in all kind of works, by means of which he will be aware of a variety of problems faced by the writers in their attempts of artistic creation. As a second safeguard the historian is required to realize the nature of poetry and criticism as assumed in this mode of critical study. These and the scattered remarks of poets from ancient to the modern age will enable the historian to realize the various artistic and technical problems faced by the artists. Crane also suggests the *Poetics* as an essential guide of the literary historian for the analysis of certain things of literary works.

The measures Crane suggests to overcome the defects of his method remind one of Eliot's insistence on the role of tradition in the education of a poet. Eliot believes that a poet in order to be a significant poet "must be very conscious of the main current, which does not at all flow invariably through the most distinguished reputations. He must be quite aware of the obvious fact that art never improves, but that the material of art is never quite the same. He must be aware that the mind of Europe—the mind of his own country, a mind which he learns in time to be much more important than his own private mind—is a mind which changes, and that this change is a development which abandons nothing *en route*, which does not superannuate either Shakespeare, or Homer, or the rock drawing of the Megdalenian draughtsmen" (Eliot *Sacred Wood* 51). Similarly Crane also suggests that a critic must have the entire Europe in his bones if he wants to do justice to his job. Although we must hasten to add, even an awareness of the great European literary tradition may not always be very effective in judging a new work of art for two reasons. First, because in spite of the widest possible critical reading a critic is a man governed by his personal passions and prejudices. Eliot also remarked in "The Frontier of Criticism" (1956), published just one year before Crane's essay on the principles of literary history: "[...] the literary critic is not merely a technical expert, who has learned the rules to be observed by the writers he criticizes: the critic must be the whole man, a man with convictions and principles, and of knowledge and experience of life" (Eliot *Poetry and Poets* 116). Secondly, a new work of art may be completely different from everything that has gone before. In such cases a critic's knowledge of the literary tradition fails him in assessing this new work of art. The point is that apart from the fact that every literary work is unique as a mode of discourse, when it breaks away from the tradition it calls for new poetics and new critical criteria for its evaluation. A work of the East, for example, an Indian poem cannot be satisfactorily judged by Western criteria. Similarly, the plays of Brecht arising out of new historical situation and sharply different German sensibility cannot be properly evaluated by Aristotelian canons. Not to speak of Brecht, even a Shakespearean play, when judged by principles laid down in the *Poetics*, throws up more points of departure than points of conformity.

Nevertheless, objectivity is an ideal worth struggling for while it is good to know the limitations under which a critic is obliged to work. He cannot abdicate his responsibility and should try to be as objective as possible. Crane is evidently fully aware of these limitations, and that is why he is so serious in trying to plug the lacunae of different schools and plead of a kind of criticism that tries to be 'as comprehensive as possible.'

After analysing the critical elements necessary to construct literary history, Crane takes up in broader perspective the task of analysing the traditional forms of literary history. One of the traditional forms of literary history is that which follows three things alone—succession in time, distribution in space, and likeness and difference in character—as its principles of organization. Most of the literary histories written so far, which survey systematically the literary productions of a nation, or of an age, or of a class of writers are of this group. Crane calls it 'atomistic history' because in this mode works or authors generally become the primary units or atoms of interpretation.

The use of the same principles of organization, however, does not mean that all the histories written under this mode will be the same. Their differences are due to the different ways the historians follow to construct the basic principles of succession, and of likeness and difference. In some histories the succession is of individual writers, whereas in some others it is of periods or ages. In the use of the principle of likeness and difference also, that is in respect of critical consideration one history differs from another. Some histories follow purely philological mode of investigation whereas the majority of others combine philological and dialectical methods in their critical findings. Crane observes that "there are few histories in this tradition that do not combine the results of philological and biographical research with their dialectical characterizations and estimates: but individual histories differ greatly according as one or the other of the two elements is made to predominate and according as the two are more or less closely related in the historian's exposition" (Crane *Literary History* 27).

In this connection we may see how literary histories of this group actually differ. Legouis and Cazamian in the general introduction to *A History of English Literature* write: "Only by forgoing any picture of literary expression overseas has it been possible to trace the history of English literature not too superficially, and to show its development coherently and harmoniously because with unity of place" (Legouis & Cazamian xiii). The avowed intention of the authors was to enable the students of English "to grasp the dominating features of succeeding periods and follow the reflection in books of the development of a great people" (Legouis & Cazamian xiii). The central aim of the authors is to present literary history as coherent and harmonious and to highlight the salient features of different periods. George Sampson, on the other hand, writes in his preface to the first edition of *The Concise Cambridge History of English Literature* in 1941: "There is always an appeal from criticism to history, which is the record, not of suppositions, but of achievements. The main purpose of this volume therefore, is to exhibit 'the progress of poesy' as something that really happened and interested many generations. The book does not offer a collection of opinions that a reader can take over ready-made. It is a guide to reading, not a substitute for reading. It represents, in the main, the general consensus of opinion." The point of difference is that while Legouis and Cazamian present history as coherent and harmonious by pointing out the dominating features of different periods, it is they who decide which features dominate, but Sampson claims to present not his view but 'the general consensus of opinion' (Sampson XI). In both these literary histories the faculty of criticism is in operation. In Legouis it operates in dovetailing the differences and in discerning the continuity of the historical forces while in Sampson it operates in assessing or distilling the report or the general consensus of opinion. But in neither case a literary history is a mechanical records of literary events. Legouis, strictly speaking, does not suffer from the defects so acutely as Crane would make us believe. We should also remember that in 1926 when Legouis and Cazamian's history was first published it was historically not possible for them to be more objective and critical than what they have been. Sampson, writing in 1941, had the advantage of the tested scholarship in the fields of both history and criticism. Already Eliot was a celebrity. More recent literary historians have been more critical in their approach. Rene Wellek has strictly conformed to the 'literary' while writing his monumental *History of Modern Criticism 1750-1950.* David Daiches's *A Critical History of English Poetry* is avowedly critical.

However, the most remarkable defect of this mode of writing literary history arises out of the simple principle of atomistic succession. The narrative in it takes a fresh start with each period or author and in consequence it loses continuity. The integrity of the history is thus, hampered. Besides, the limitations of the philological and dialectical modes of critical investigation are also there.

Attempts have been made to avoid the defects of the atomistic history in another form of literary history in which the integration has been effected, in a great many ways, in terms of the connection between literature and other things. Crane calls it integral or organic literary history.

Different types of integral histories have been written. Crane mentions Leavis's *Revaluation* and Brooks's *Notes for a Revised History of English Poetry* as examples of the general class of integral history where, in the language of Crane, "the unity is achieved by the application to successive writers of a single dialect of combination and separation having as its elements a compendent set of 'literary' qualities or values, the necessity pervading the history being that of the disjunctive major premise of critical theory which holds it together" (Crane *Literary History* 29). In some other variety writers or their works are characterized in terms of their various expressions or reflections of a single line of development in the general life of the time. A third variety of integral history is seen in the attempts of writing literary history in terms of Marxist theory. This group of historians assume that literary works must inevitably be reflections of their age and so they make the political or economic structure of society as the primary determinant. Bateson's *English Poetry: A Critical Introduction* is an attempt of this type of history.

Various modes of organic history solve the problems of continuity and relevance—the qualities which the atomistic history lacks. In lieu of the simple chronological succession of the atomistic history, organic history follows a logical progression of schematism of ideas. Thus the problem of continuity is solved and all the writers of all species of works are connected analogically by means of some common terms and distinctions applied to all of them.

But the historians of this mode with an eye to remove the limitations of atomistic history, fall a victim to some other defects. The dialectical method which almost all the varieties of integral history exercise tend to reduce literary modes to certain social, political, linguistic or intellectual terms. Thus, the history of literature may ultimately be moral history of the society it reflects. What is even more serious is that the dialectical reduction which the historians of this mode use, submerge the individual traits of literary works to a great extent into the abstractions of the unifying scheme. The history very often loses its true character and sounds like philosophy. And the question of making sense out of the literary past will lose its significance because the individual and peculiar features which express themselves through different works are not exposed.

Thus Crane finds both the traditional methods of writing literary history defective. And this observation leads him to construct a less defective, if not absolutely perfect, method. He calls it 'the narrative history of literary forms.' The model of such a history has been the narrative causal sequences, not dialectical analysis of causal factors. Its principles are some general factors implicit in any instance of change. They are as Crane suggests: "(a) an initial situation from which the change proceeds; (b) a final situation in which the first situation eventuates and which contrasts with the first in kind, quality, or amount; (c) a continuing matter which undergoes change and of which both end terms can be predicted and (d) a moving cause, or convergence of moving causes, capable of bringing about the particular change defined by the other variables" (Crane *Literary History* 33).

Some particular attempts have been made to deal narratively with literary phenomena. But their chief limitations emerge from the critical principles employed in discriminating the changing characteristics of works. They depend largely on grammatical statements about the form and content of works. Naturally they lack the fullest literary particularity and possible adequacy of historical explanation. So Crane proposes an extension and refinement of narrative literary history on the basis of the concept of artistic synthesis—the critical concept which is often found absent in most histories. The historian should, Crane suggests, write a narrative causal history of literary arts in terms of four things: (a) the successive changes in artistic or formal ends, (b) changes in materials, (c) changes in the techniques of writers and (d) the successive actualization of all these changing possibilities in the production of artistically valuable works with which the history deals. Crane considers the first element—the element of form—to be of prior importance because the two others—material and technique—are dependent on or fully explicable in a particular work only by reference to the form. Here one must remember the distinction between the mechanical form and the organic form. The mechanical form anticipates the structure and predetermines it. The organic form develops from within and is determined by the potentialities inherent in the 'seeds' of a literary work. Crane is right to call this history the narrative history of forms. However, the crucial problems of the historian in this mode are (a) to discriminate the different artistic ends which the writers pursue from time to time, and (b) to organize the differences into some significant lines of change. In other words the basic elements of a work—the elements of form, material and technique—must not merely be examined separately, but they must be combined in some way. So Crane inquires into the kind of causal efficacy which may be assumed to bind literary events and changes together.

Unlike the historian of the organic type of history whose general preference is to select one type of causality, the historian of forms makes provisions for all type of causal problems. He has to maintain at least two levels of causation--constructional and preconstructional. And as the consideration of the preconstructional causes cannot be done without analysing the problems or causes involved in actual construction, the historian's first inquiry is into the constructional causes. Crane observes that the artist in the process of construction finds some devices of plot, diction or characterization unfit, whereas some others essential. The artist must know why he selects some devices to achieve his whole. And these reasons will constitute artistic or poetic causes for the historian, who is required to explain the reasons.

Here we must note that the type of inquiry the historian is

required to make regarding the constructional causes is bound to be subjective. The historian can only guess but not confirm the type of reasons actually operative in the mind of the artist. Any systematic attempt to do so would lead us to what is known as psychoanalytic criticism of the author. But such criticism takes the interest away from the work to the author. The importance of the work there consists only as a manifestation of the psychology of the artist. Such approach is not, in the strict sense, literary; it is psychological. There is, in fact, no objective method to judge these reasons and to confirm that they are the actual reasons of artistic construction. Naturally the chance of wrong judgment lurks all the time. But it must be admitted that the historian will be better equipped to assess properly the aspects of a poetic production if the artistic causes of that production become clear to him.

However, the historian of form is also required to consider two extra-poetic causes—one stemming from the author's extra-formal aims, and the other from the condition set for him by his conception of his readers or critics, the occasion of his writing, the peculiar nature of his materials, and his personal situations at the time.

There is, however, a relation between the artistic or poetic causes and extra-poetic causes. A relation is also there between the constructional and the preconstructional causes. The least remote preconstructional cause is the author himself, that is to mean the biographical elements. But the approach of the historian of forms is different from that of the biographical critic. The biographical critic begins by conjecturing the nature of an author's private interests, moral problems etc. from his letters and other records, and then analyse the literary works in the light of those findings, but the historian of forms is required to proceed from the works to the biographical findings of the man.

The causal problems of the historian of forms, Crane observes, become complex enough when he attempts to analyse historically the causes of the great collective events like the development and decline of the 'metaphysical' tradition in poetry. The historians of other schools have suggested various easy solutions to such problems. Any traditional historian, for example, may hold such an opinion that the cause of the complexities in technique and form of modern poetry is "the methods of modern science or the disappearance of formerly common beliefs from modern life" (Crane *Literary History* 79). But the historian of forms can hardly accept such causes. He can consider as causes only those events which can be connected with the literary effects by showing their direct or indirect operation in the productive acts of the writers in question. He must be convinced that (i) his causal propositions are clearly and sufficiently explained, (ii) they are appropriate to the effects they are intended to clarify, and (iii) they are commensurate with the effects.

The traditional historians often fall victim to such a wrong assumption that causal propositions must be general in case of certain general facts. Facts are general in the sense that the writers of certain age, the metaphysical poets or the romantics for example, share a general outlook or thought and exploit certain materials or techniques commonly. They are thus tempted to introduce some descriptive chapters in their histories on the background of the literature of a period. The historian of forms suspects such hypotheses because they discourage sufficient inquiry into the more immediate formal and extra-formal factors.

Another thing Crane observes in this context is that the principles of art in general and the pronouncements of critics often affect or tend to affect the practice of writers. But this point has hardly been used convincingly in the casual interpretation of literary events in any history. Actually the difficulty of the literary historian is that he cannot clearly determine, even when he discovers clear affinities between a particular literary work and certain critical rules favoured in that age, how far the work is an outcome of the influence of those critical observation. Crane desires the historian of forms to be well aware of the different complexities which may arise in regard to the relation between criticism and literary productions. "He (the historian of forms) will approach any possible influence of this kind from the point of view not of what he knows concerning the history of doctrines but of his prior analysis of the artistic problems which his writers faced because of their choices of formal ends" (Crane *Literary History* 89). The problem that Crane thought about was partly envisaged by Eliot in his essay "Johnson as Critic and Poet," published in 1944. Eliot calls attention to "the critic's failure to apply his own standards from those apparent errors which spring from the principles of a particular mind at a particular time, and which no longer seem to us errors in the same sense, once we succeed in apprehending the point of view" (Eliot *Poetry and Poets* 117). But while Eliot shows an awareness of the problem only, Crane goes a step forward and offers some concrete suggestions for tackling, if not overcoming, this problem.

Some greater problems are faced by historians in their attempt to deal with society, which is supposed rightly to be the cause of many literary effects. It is often enthusiastically said that literature is an expression of society. The historian of forms also does not treat literature in abstraction from life. But he also believes that there can be an artist who turns his mind away from politics or economics and concentrates purely on the artistic problems. In other words, reflection of social awareness, according to Crane, is not a necessary condition of good literary work.

With respect to the causal investigation the method which the historian of forms follows is an analytical method presupposing for all literary events a multiplicity of distinguishable causes. The peculiar forms or powers of individual works in this method are determined by the specifically different principles of construction their writers have used. And the primary task of the historian is to define the various forms, which writers have achieved more or less successfully.

The objection which is sometimes raised against this mode of literary history is, Crane says, that "it tends to obscure or distort the nature of the facts the historian is studying by directing attention separately to causal factors which in their actual operation are inseparable" (Crane *Literary History* 106). There is truth in it and Crane admits that this is of course a defect of this method. But in comparison to the defects in other methods it is less harmful. And Crane without trying to vindicate this charge insists that the best thing for the historian to follow is to push his analytical inquiries as far as they can go. It surely indicates Crane's fine sense of pragmatism.

6

CRANE AND THE HISTORY OF IDEAS

An important part of Crane's belief is that the history of ideas is 'a good thing' for both the literary artists and the literary critics and scholars. Literary artists, whether consciously or not, exploit ideas which appear in various forms in their works. Most of the 18th century writers for example, as Crane shows in his essay "Suggestions Toward a Genealogy of the 'Man of Feeling,'" were more or less influenced by the 'man of feeling' cult, and in consequence the mid-eighteenth century literature was full of sentimental heroes and heroines. Literary critics and scholars are also required to have a definite knowledge of the history of ideas. Otherwise it will be difficult for them to properly understand, illustrate and evaluate ideas expressed in literature. Crane's belief, I think, is shared by others also.

In his *The Idea of the Humanities and Other Essays, Critical and Historical, Vol. I* Crane has grouped five essays, written in different times and on different occasions, under the generalised heading of "The History of Ideas." The essays included under this title are (i) "Suggestions Toward a Genealogy of the 'Man of Feeling'" (1934), (ii) "Anglican Apologetics and the Idea of Progress, 1699-1745" (1934), (iii) "Montesquieu and British Thought: Gibbon, Adam Smith, Burke" (1941), (iv) "Philosophy, Literature, and the History of Ideas" (1954) and (v) "Notes on the Organization of Locke's 'Essay'" (1965). Crane's aim in these essays is not to construct a history of the ideas. In each of the essays he has considered some different, or we may say independent, problems or objects of interest. In one essay, for example, he tries to identify the distinctive nature of literary ideas, whereas in another he concerns himself with the origin and development of a particular idea—its historical background and the ways of its coming into vogue. Thus, each essay of this group deals with different problems. Of course, they are related to one another in the sense that the problems Crane tries to solve in these essays are all related to the history of ideas. Still each one is independent and complete in itself. That is why Crane does not follow chronology in arranging them in his book.

Another important thing to note in this context is that these five essays are not all that Crane says about ideas. We must include at least one more essay, namely, his "Interpretation of Texts and the History of Ideas," in which Crane considers the necessity of a successful cultivation of the history of ideas and the difficulties in such a cultivation. One may also mention Crane's "The Houyhnhnms, the Yahoos, and the History of Ideas" as another writing in the related subject. And surely this essay also has its contribution to any illustration of Crane's view on the history of ideas. But I shall keep this particular essay out of the purview of my discussion at present for two reasons. One is that this essay is primarily an example of practical criticism. It exhibits Crane as a practising critic and contains only a little amount of theory. The other reason is that I am going to consider this essay on the fourth voyage of *Gulliver's Travels* separately in my next chapter along with other examples of Crane's practical criticism. So, for the time being, I shall try to illustrate the remaining six essays on the history of ideas showing how they mark Crane's originality of critical insight as well as what they exhibit about his impression on the subject.

I

SUGGESTIONS TOWARD A GENEALOGY OF THE 'MAN OF FEELING'

In the literature and philosophical writings of the mid-eighteenth century the abundance of sentimentalism is quite discernible. The distinguishing notes of the philosophical expressions of that period were, to quote R.S. Crane, "The identification of virtue with acts of benevolence and still more with the feelings of universal goodwill which inspire and accompany these acts; the assumption that such 'good Affections' are the natural and spontaneous growth of the heart of man uncorrupted by habits of vice" (Crane *Humanities* Vol. I 189). Besides, the literary artists of the 18th century modelled their heroes and heroines of countless English novels, poems and plays after the philosophical concepts of sentimental feelings, benevolence, moral weeping and good affections. All these exhibit unmistakably that the mid-eighteenth century generated and popularized the cult of the 'man of feeling.' Sentimentalism became one of the chief aspects of literature of that time.

The debatable issue, however, is not the cult itself, but its origin. How did it come to triumph during the 18th century when "neither in antiquity, nor in the Middle Ages, nor in the sixteenth century, nor in the England of the Puritans and Cavaliers had the 'man of feeling' ever been a popular type" (Crane *Humanities* Vol. I 190)? Crane in his essay "Suggestions Toward a Genealogy of the 'Man of Feeling'" tries to answer this question.

A solution to the problem of origin of the 'man of feeling' cult has been accepted by many scholars. They take it for granted that the writings of the third Earl of Shaftesbury and his followers were there as inspirations behind the moulding up of sentimentalism. For, truly speaking, the distinctive traits of the 'man of feeling' cult are found to exist in the writings of Shaftesbury and his followers, which were published in the early part of the 18th century.

Crane, however, refuses to give full credit to Shaftesbury and his followers on the ground that their writings appeared too late. He tries to trace it out in some philosophical and religious writings of the previous century. He believes that it is not in the influence of any single moralist like Shaftesbury but in "the combined influence of numerous Anglican divines of the Latitudinarian tradition who from the Restoration onward into the eighteenth century had preached" (Crane *Humanities* Vol. I 190) the same ethics of benevolence, that the real source of the 18th century cult of sensibility can be found. In support of his belief Crane has mentioned four major aspects of the ethical and psychological preaching of these divines.

The first remarkable aspect of their preaching was to equate virtue with universal benevolence. They had actually before them the hope of freeing religion from the darker aspects of the Puritan creed. That was why they insisted on the humane qualities like love, benevolence and good-feeling. This type of humanitarian homiletic of the Latitudinarian school was delivered to the public since about 1680s and it became stronger than ever in the early 18th century. Long before Shaftesbury people came to know from Samuel Clarke that "the true End and Design of Religion, is manifestly this; to make Men wiser and better; to improve, exalt and perfect their Nature; to teach them to obey, and love, and imitate God; to cause them to extend their love and Goodness and charity to all their Fellow creatures, each in their several stations, and according to the measure of their several Abilities; in like manner as the universal Goodness of God Extends itself over all his works through the whole Creation" (Clarke 2).

The second aspect of their preaching was that they attached 'benevolence' to 'tender human feelings.' True benevolence, according to them, is that which springs from tender feelings of pity and compassion, and therefore one should try to develop those feelings within oneself instead of suppressing them. Their repeated emphasis on the elements of 'tenderness' and quick response to the misery of man gradually leads to the conception of the 18th century 'man of feeling.' Crane has cited passages from the writings of Robert South, Gregory Hascard, William Sherlock and other anti-stoic preachers of the later 1600s to show the growing urge for sentimentalism. The most distinguishing mark of the benevolent man, as these writers emphasized, is that he must feel for others. And this quality of human mind (ability to feel) is there in the background of the terms like 'moral weeping' and 'sensibility' which were used by the sentimentalists of the 18th century to eulogize the quality of mind.

Another important thing the anti-stoical divines preached was that benevolent feelings are quite natural to man. They pictured human heart as naturally good, and disseminated the view that it tends invariably to tender human feelings.

The last important thing that contributed to the formation of the popular 18th century conception on the 'man of feeling' was the preaching of the divines that the benevolent emotions afford joy to those who feel them. This idea of receiving joy in exchange of exercising benevolent emotions was perhaps received from Aristotle and moulded by the divines to suit their purpose. It was also prevalent in the Elizabethan period. In Shakespeare's *The Merchant of Venice*, for example, it has been said that the reward of being merciful is an experience of joy. Crane has quoted Tillotson and Parker to show that they have estimated the pleasure in doing good to be greater than any sensual pleasure in the world. All these writings created a sense of the greatness of tender feelings and emotional expressions in the minds of the public, which ultimately formed and popularized the 'man of feeling' cult of the mid-18th century.

Thus Crane studies the tradition of the Latitudinarian divines to ascertain the cause of the 18th century sentimentalism. Crane, however, does not deny the influence of Shaftesbury and his followers. He rather considers it to be an effective influence toward the formation of this cult especially after 1725. His only claim is that his study of the writings of the Latitudinarian clergymen will help to make the whole movement of the 'man of feeling' more intelligible. This attitude of Crane is quite in tune with his anti-monistic critical temperament. And, truly speaking Crane's explanations widen the range of information, which will certainly enable the scholars to approach the problem from different standpoints.

II

"ANGLICAN APOLOGETICS AND THE IDEA OF PROGRESS, 1699-1745"

In "Anglican Apologetics and the Idea of Progress, 1699-1745" Crane studies the contribution of the Anglican divines to the formation of the progressivist myth. The progressivist myth—a belief in the theory that the history of civilization is an account of constant progress and that man, as he gathers experiences, passes from worse to better—chiefly gathered its force from the Enlightenment. The scientists, philosophers, and literary artists who looked forward for a hopeful future had the greatest contribution in diffusing the theory of progress. But Crane considers it to be only a part of the picture. He believes that a group of other writers has also a great contribution toward formulation and dissemination of the theory of progress, especially in England. They were the orthodox Anglican divines who were quite active in the first half of the 18th century and who exploited the theory of progress in their own way to protect revealed religion from the attacks of its enemies. They found that the theory of progress might help them to answer some of the embarrassing questions of the deists and others who suspected the greatness and appropriateness of Christianity. Crane here considers the writings of John Edwards, William Worthington and Edmund Law, the three great contributors to the progressivist doctrine, in some details to show how these divines explained and popularized the idea in the 18th century England.

Edwards was the pioneer to the movement. He draws a very consistent and elaborate picture of the constant progress of religious state toward perfection in future. With the help of his imagination he depicts the happiest age of mankind. Crane admits that Edwards's approach was modernist because he attached religious progressivism to that of science and philosophy.

Edwards's explanations, however, have two major lapses. Firstly, Crane has rightly suggested that the modernism of Edwards was more assumed than real, because he failed to free himself from the illusion of the Golden Age; the traditional belief in the existence of that age was retained in his writing. Secondly, Edwards failed to make credible his picture of the future perfect world. He only played upon imagination and could hardly convince us why and how the future world must be as he had imagined.

However, after Edwards William Worthington came forward to carry on the type of apologetic Edwards had started. Worthington had before him two purposes to fulfil. One was of course to vindicate Christianity against the attack of the deists, and the other was to solve the problem of the natural and moral evils introduced into the world as a result of the Fall. As a follower of Edwards, Worthington also depicted "the main steps in man's gradual redemption from the antediluvian age to the end of the world" (Crane *Humanities* Vol. I 246). But his notion of the perfect state of mankind at the end of progress is different from Edwards's. He speculates the future moral and religious state to be the same as it was for a short time at the beginning. Worthington here commits a gross mistake which Crane has only hinted but not elaborated. His identification of the future state of perfection with the earliest is quite incongruous with the theory of progress. If we are to believe as the previous theologists made us believe that God blesses us with gradual prosperity, then the conception of the perfect state of the world at the beginning loses its credibility. And if we were to believe in the existence of the perfect state at the beginning, which was comparable with the future state of perfection, then the theory of progress leads us to no forward journey but only to a backward movement. However, it must be admitted that Worthington deserves a remarkable position among the antideistic writers. His Essay acted as a "fresh emphasis to the growing belief that later times are bound to be superior on the whole to earlier, not only in knowledge of nature and mechanical skill, but also in spiritual insight and moral excellence" (Crane *Humanities* Vol. I 250).

The next important name in the tradition of antideistic writing is Edmund Law, whose book was some sort of a reply to the agitation caused by the publication of Matthew Tindal's *Christianity as Old as the Creation*. Tindal's attack on religion was on the ground that whatever is true or valuable must be characterized by universality of diffusion and appeal. Christianity lacks these qualities. It appeared late and is still now confined to only a part of the world, and therefore it can hardly claim to be the true religion. In his reply to this attack Law based his arguments on psychological grounds and maintained that God's desire was not to offer complete perfection and absolute happiness to man at a time. Human beings must prepare themselves through experiences before receiving the blessings of God. Drawing examples from nature he justifies that everything on earth grows to perfection gradually. In case of religion also it cannot be otherwise. Law actually did a lot in his earnest desire to answer Tindal, and formulated what Crane calls "a theory of the progressive religious and moral education of the human race" (Crane *Humanities* Vol. I 271-72). His greatest contribution is that he was the first to introduce the psychological theories to justify progressivism in religious history.

Crane has also considered a few minor writers who appeared after 1745 to exhibit that the idea of progress was a dominant theme in their articles and books. And from his consideration of all these writers he sums up the nature of the movement in England in a few points. First, the Anglican writers throughout the first half of the 18th century developed their distinctive theory of general progress and popularized it in England. The influences coming from France were felt only after 1750 and that was also greatly exaggerated. His second observation is that "in the formulation of this theory before 1750 the determining factors were mainly of a religious nature" (Crane *Humanities* Vol. I 286). And those who gave a particular shape to this new philosophy were, unlike those in France, the friends to the church. These divines were, again, motivated not by any philosophical insight but by the urgent need of protecting revealed religion against the deists. But gradually the optimistic people gave it the shape of an independent philosophical doctrine of the 18th century. Another point Crane draws in this connection is that in England Edmund Law was the most prominent figure of the movement. It was he who popularized the theory among the educated public by means of his attractive and inventing manner of arguing.

However, this essay thus explores one yet unexplored realm of the progressivist movement. The writings of the Anglican divines were surely there, but none attempted the type of historical investigation Crane has completed here to point out the contribution of the Anglican divines toward formulation of the theory of constant progress.

III

"MONTESQUIEU AND BRITISH THOUGHT: GIBBON, ADAM SMITH, BURKE

In the article "Montesquieu and British Thought:Gibbon, Adam Smith, Burke" we find R.S. Crane as a book-reviewer. Crane reviews Fletcher's book *Montesquieu and English Politics (1750-1800)*—the book in which Fletcher has attempted to show how a large number of great and small historians, economists, political orators and even constitutionalist theorists of the 2nd half of the 18th century exploited Montesquieu's *Esprit des lois* for material assistance or support of their own arguments. Fletcher shows the likeness of thoughts between Montesquieu on the one hand and a group of English writers on the other. The method he follows for this purpose is a comparative one. And Crane observes that Fletcher is most successful when he argues on the philological level and exhibits the influence of Montesquieu on the British writers through a simple comparison of texts and doctrines. But whenever his observation moves beyond that field and Crane has pointed out that Fletcher moves time and again, and whenever "his judgments take the form of generalizations about the fundamental procedures of his authors or the implications of their statements" (Crane *Humanities* Vol. I 303), he can fairly be acused of oversimplifying the problems occurring in the authors he deals with due to his failure to understand properly the principles underlying their works. In his article Crane first points to the limitations of Fletcher's understanding of Montesquieu and then to his lack of understanding of relation of other writers to Montesquieu. Regarding Fletcher's understanding of *Esprit des lois* Crane observes that Fletcher's interpretation of the book is done in Platonic terms. It is, however, not wrong to interpret *Esprit des lois* in Platonic terms. Crane rather admits the validity of that interpretation. But he, at the same time, does not hesitate to mention that it is not the proper way since to understand the book in the way Fletcher does is to "neglect the distinction Montesquieu establishes in Book I between laws 'in their most general signification,' which are necessary relations arising from the 'nature' or the *raison primitive* of things, and laws in the sense of rules established by legislators using their 'human reason' or faculty adjusting means to ends in a world of finite beings and varying physical and social conditions. It is with 'law' and 'reason' in the second of these senses that Montesquieu is primarily concerned" (Crane *Humanities* Vol. I 303-04). What Crane thus suggests is that Fletcher's tendency to generalizing keeps him away from a more careful, analytical study of Montesquieu.

The same charge can be brought against Fletcher in his attempt to study the influence of Montesquieu on English writers. Crane mentions only three of the English writers—Gibbon, Adam Smith and Burke—to give us an example of Fletcher's dealing with them. Fletcher for example , Crane observes, fails to have a clear understanding of Gibbon and the nature of the influence of Montesquieu on him. Fletcher insists on Gibbon's neglect of general for particular causes in his account of the greatness of Rome. Crane has analysed the point to show how Fletcher has achieved a wrong judgment. Crane observes: "The point is not that he (Gibbon) is neglecting general causes but that, given the essential nature of a despotism, however disguised, the happiness or misery of the Commonwealth must necessarily be dependent, as he recognizes at the end of Chapter 3, on the character of a single man" (Crane *Humanities* Vol. I 307). Crane also exhibits that the way Gibbon did his analysis in chapter 3 of his book was largely due to the influence of Book XI of *Esprit des lois* in which Montesquieu expounded the theory of balance and separation of powers in his account of the British constitution. Fletcher misses the point and thus fails to do justice to the influence of Montesquieu on Gibbon.

Similarly, in his treatment of Adam Smith also, Crane has exhibited, Fletcher exaggerates the intellectual relation between Montesquieu and Smith. Of course, Crane admits Fletcher's success in pointing out Montesquieu's influence on Burke. Fletcher, Crane observes, is right in his attempts to show that many of the arguments in different books and articles of Burke are linked to *Esprit des lois.* But at the same time Crane criticises Fletcher for making some generalised statements in order to differentiate Burke's political approach from that of Montesquieu.

However, Crane in this review article has remained confined to these three writers only. He says nothing about how Fletcher exhibits the influence of Montesquieu on other writers of England. It may be due to the fact that Crane thinks it enough to make us understand the basic approach of Fletcher in his book, and to do so three writers of three major fields of study are sufficient. Besides, the duty of a reviewer is not to summarize the whole book but to point out the major traits and to evaluate the achievement of the writer. Crane's article seems to support this view. And there can hardly be any doubt that Crane has successfully performed this task of a reviewer.

IV

"PHILOSOPHY, LITERATURE, AND THE HISTORY OF IDEAS"

A very interesting as well as important essay of Crane is "Philosophy, Literature, and the History of Ideas," where he examines the nature and function of literary ideas "in the context both of ideas in philosophy and of ideas in the history of ideas" (Crane *Humanities* Vol. I 173). The essay can be divided into two parts for the sake of understanding—the first dealing with the nature of ideas occurring in the history of ideas, philosophy and literature along with a few suggestions on the construction of the history of ideas, and the second showing the applications and roles of the ideas in literary works, on the basis of which an idea becomes literary.

The history of ideas, Crane observes, works on a large canvas. For the purpose of its working materials the history of ideas is not restricted to any particular branch of knowledge, but can easily exploit philosophy, literature, theology, history, scientific treatise and, what not, because ideas in different forms may be traced in all the established branches of knowledge. But the history of ideas does not entertain the ideas as they appear in various fields because the same idea may and does assume different outward forms and implications as it occurs in different fields. The scholar's job, therefore, is of "separating out from particular systems of thought, viewed as more or less unstable 'compounds,' the basic conceptual and methodological elements of which they are composed, and the results of this analysis—the 'unit ideas' it fixes our attention on—become the essential data of the history of ideas" (Crane *Humanities* Vol. I 173). The term 'unit ideas' has been borrowed from A.O. Lovejoy, and 'unit ideas' are the basic ideas which frequently occur in speeches and writings of scholars of different fields. They are thus universal notions, which work in the minds of writers as well as scholars. And this universality of thought actually makes us often surprisingly discover the affinity of ideas between the writers of two different countries or between two writings of widely different natures. Crane uses the term 'commmonplaces' to mean what Lovejoy calls 'unit ideas' because he considers it more comprehensive.

However, these ideas are of immense value for the interpretation of philosophical and literary works as well as others. So the historical study of ideas, Crane rightly observes, should be done with care and interest. And he has scholastically showed that this can be done in three different ways. The first one can be called a Text-oriented study of the ideas. The historian may take as his working material any literary or philosophical text and then he shows how the author of the text has exploited the 'commonplaces' or 'unit ideas' available to him in earlier writings. The other way of studying ideas may be seen as a diachronic study of an idea. In this process a historian may take up some idea in isolation and then show the gradual development and implications of the idea through examples from different fields and different periods as long as the idea remains current. And the third method may be called a synchronic or period oriented study of ideas. Here one is required to concentrate one's attention on a particular period and then to closely examine and show what ideas predominate in that period, occurring in different provinces of thought.

The task, however, is by no means an easy one. Some problems are there in each of the methods. The first problem is to identify the ideas because the task must be done from artistic or scholastic writings in which the ideas appear in a wide variety of forms. The same idea may and does take different names after the names of the fields in which they are employed. Thus the ideas appearing in philosophy are called philosophical ideas, in literature, literary ideas. The historian must have to recognize the basic ideas free from all the outer formative decorations they receive in a particular branch of knowledge—say for example, literature or philosophy. Another equally serious task is to study how and why one idea or a group of ideas predominates in a particular period and how it gives place to another.

Crane next turns to the other object of his interest in this article, namely, the identification of the distinctive nature of literary ideas. He rightly observes that most of the serious literary works possess within themselves some philosophical truths. The thoughts expressed in those works often become similar to some remarkable ideas occurring in some philosophical writings. This incident never suggests that literary ideas are identical with philosophical ideas. Actually philosophical ideas often recur in literature, but their forms and implications very often change as they undergo or sometimes help literary synthesis. So in order to recognize the peculiarly literary ideas "we must consider them in the light of the literary synthesis they help to make possible and of their various functions relative to these" (Crane *Humanities* Vol. I 183). But the problem here is that literary synthesis takes place in no fixed, or one or two ways. Naturally, one engaged in examining the parts played by ideas in literary synthesis must explore all the possible varieties.

However, Crane has also observed that the role of ideas varies as widely as the literary structures vary. In the structure, for example, where metaphor and analogy play an important part, ideas are often used as bases of the metaphors and analogies. In the dramatic structures "the dramatis personae are frequently made to state universal propositions or to develop generalized arguments in order that their estimates of the situation, their motives in the action, their plans and deliberations may be clear" (Crane *Humanities* Vol. I 184). In some other structures again, ideas are used as "external signs or manifestations of inner moral habits and states of mind" (Crane *Humanities* Vol. I 185). The soliloquies of Hamlet may be cited as examples. Thus, in various structures ideas play various roles.

The role of the ideas, however, is more artistic than philosophical, and they play mainly some functional parts in all such structures. Another important thing Crane suggests here is that in most of the representational works we often search and generally find certain 'universally intelligible postulates,' wherefrom we constitute an idea of the 'vision of life' or 'world-view' of the author. These postulates are generally implied in the structure but not clearly stated, and they may be traced to be the reflection of some philosophical or theological systems.

What finally emerges from Crane's investigation of the nature of literary ideas is that they are used in literary works in two principal ways: (i) as moral and intellectual bases of their forms and (ii) as parts or devices necessitated or made appropriate by their forms. And naturally there can be no single way of judging the significance of ideas used in literature. The criterion must be changed as we take up either of the functions of the ideas. It may passingly be noted here that this idea of changing the criterion or method as and when necessary is fundamental in Crane's critical theory.

A very important point that Crane makes at the end of the article is that the material of ideas in a literary work does not determine the greatness of that work. The peculiarly literary value of literature depends on the pleasure it affords as a 'beautiful individual whole,' constituted of so many materials. Therefore, a merely philosophical consideration (in the traditional way) of the ideas involved in literature is never sufficient because the ideas here achieve something more than merely philosophical significance.

V

"NOTE ON THE ORGANIZATION OF LOCKE'S ESSAY"

Crane's concern here is to point out the main design of Locke's *Essay Concerning Human Understanding*. His professed aim is twofold—one is to study the character of the basic analogy which, Crane thinks, is there at the centre of Locke's *Essay*, and the other is to examine how far this unifying analogy controls the movement of Locke's arguments throughout the *Essay*.

Locke in his *Essay* records the "history of the first beginnings of human knowledge." The function of the human mind is extremely vital in the production of knowledge and therefore, Locke first determines the nature and function of the mind. He does it by means of an analogy which, Crane thinks, is basic to Locke's analysis in his *Essay*. In the first chapter of the second Book of the *Essay* Locke informs us that thinking or perception of ideas is related to the soul in the same way as motion is related to the body. Here Locke differs from the Cartesians in his concept of the soul. Unlike the Cartesians, who consider thinking or perception of ideas to be essence of the soul, Locke takes it to be just one of the activities of the soul. And this activity of the soul, Locke thinks, can fully be analysed by means of the same terms used to consider physical activity. Thus Locke comes to the conclusion that both motion and thought (a) are things which have their existence in succession, (b) are diverse in nature, and (c) can both be considered in terms of the cause-effect relationship.

With the help of this analogy as a basis Locke composes "a systematic 'history' of human knowledge as something that comes to be, in a temporal and causal succession, as a result of the powers with which God has endowed the human mind" (Crane *Humanities* Vol. I 290). New things may come into being in at least three ways. But human mind in the process of converting ideas into knowledge follows mainly one of these three, and this one is the process of 'making.' Locke observes: "When the cause is extrinsical, and the effect produced by a sensible separation, or juxtaposition of discernible parts, we call it making, and such are all artificial things" (Locke 293). Human knowledge is the product of an activity of making, and the extrinsical cause here is the mind, which in Locke's concept functions like a workman or artist. Therefore, in order to explain the powers and limitations of the mind Locke draws a parallel between the activity of the mind with simple ideas and the activity of a workman with material objects. Thus, Crane shows that this fundamental analogy of Locke's book is the organizing force in the light of which, when we explain or try to understand the book, everything becomes more evident.

Since the *Essay* is a history of human knowledge, it must have its own principles of organization and interpretation. Its principles are derived from the universal traits of the mind—its powers and its situation. And these traits of the mind are determined by means of the analogy of the activity of the mind in thinking and the activity of the artist in dealing with his materials. The workman receives his materials from the world and fashions them in his own way. In this act of fashioning, certain things are active and certain others passive, some things are internal and some others external. One who attempts a study of the origin of knowledge must carefully determine the proportions of passive and active, internal and external. Crane has rightly observed that "to consider the origin of knowledge in terms of this parallel is inevitably to be led to discover in each phase of the mind's operations proportions between what is external in the process and what is internal, between what is passive and what is active; and it is precisely these proportions, applied in context after context throughout the *Essay*, that provide Locke with the general analogical framework within which his literal treatment of ideas and knowledge is developed" (Crane *Humanities* Vol. I 293). Crane, by referring to the different Books of the *Essay* has exhibited that Locke had to depend at every stage of his analysis on the determination of the ratios.

In Book I, for example, Locke has exhibited that the materials with which the mind operates have their origin, like that of the materials of the artist or the workman, in everything other than the mind. "They are," in the language of Crane, "ideas to which the understanding is related as an 'extrinsical' cause. What is internal here is only man's reason considered at once as a set of powers and as a *tabula rasa* with respect to whatever is knowable in the world" (Crane *Humanities* Vol. I 293).

The analysis in Book II also is guided by the ratio of the external materials coming within the mind and the internal operations by which these materials, the simple ideas, are made complex and made available for knowledge. Thus the proportions of active and passive, voluntary and involuntary, simple and complex, external and internal, materials of thought and the process are all involved as devices in the treatment of Locke's subject matter in the *Essay*. And the important point, to repeat it once again, is that the fundamental analogy is there as the source of all such devices.

However, in the concluding part of his essay Crane has pointed out a probable fault in the theory of Locke. He suggests that the way in which the general ideas of things are formed may ultimately obscure the original materials out of which the construction of the ideas has been made possible. And if it actually happens the extent of knowledge becomes narrow and limited because then "we can have only those notions which can be resolved ultimately into the simple ideas given us by experience; no other conceptions of sensible qualities than what come from without by the senses, no ideas of the operations of any thinking substance except those the mind finds in itself through reflection" (Crane *Humanities* Vol. I 298-99). But it must be mentioned that Locke has emphasized not the limits but the extent of human knowledge. Here Crane virtually harks back to what he said in the beginning of the essay, that Locke's view of the mind as "a passive recipient of impressions from without or at most a mechanical manipulator of the simple ideas it has derived from these" (Crane *Humanities* Vol. I 289), is extremely narrow. This approach of Crane does not do justice to Locke, because Locke's view of the mind and theory of knowledge when seen in proper perspective shows a distinct possibility of inclusiveness. Locke is often regarded as the founder of empiricism which is the doctrine that all our knowledge is derived from experience. The first book of the *Essay* is concerned in arguing as against Plato, Descartes and the scholastics that there are no innate ideas or principles. But in the second book he tries to show in detail how experience can give birth to various kinds of ideas. He rejects the notion of 'innate ideas' and contends: "Let us then suppose the mind to be, as we say, white paper, void of all characters, without any ideas; how comes it to be furnished? Whence comes it by that vast store, which the busy and boundless fancy of man has pointed on it with an almost endless variety? Whence has it all the materials of reason and knowledge? To this I answer in one word, from experience: in that all our knowledge is founded, and from that it ultimately derives itself" (Locke Chap. I, Sec. 2). Locke also makes provision for intuitive knowledge of which the mind is capable. While it is true as Crane argues that intuitive knowledge cannot be put forward in the form of logical proposition, it is also true that the intuitive knowledge is a valid form of knowledge. In fact, our knowledge of our own existence is intuitive, as Locke clearly demonstrates in book IV, while our knowledge of God's existence is demonstrative and our knowledge of things present to sense is through sensation. Obviously Crane here underestimates Locke and does injustice to him by not studying him in depth.

The mind actually has a great power of multiplying the objects of its thought and by virtue of that it can carry human knowledge much further to ensure satisfaction and happiness in this world. In fact when Locke says that the mind "in making its complex ideas of substances, only follows nature," he talks about the human limitations of the mind as an instrument. It is the human quality to join dissimilar objects in imagination but as Locke suggests, both the objects are available in experience. If we think of a golden apple which does not exist, we can think of it because we have experience of the apple and gold. All that the mind does is to connect them arbitrarily. Locke therefore makes a very significant point and strikingly original suggestion that even the concept of utopia or dystopia must take its origin in our experience of external phenomena. The mind can only recreate new objects through different permutations and combinations, but cannot really create anything *exnihilo.* But the mind has an infinite capacity of thus creating innumerable objects which do not exist in the world. Coleridge, in fact, partly draws on this quality of the mind when he talks about the esemplastic power of the mind in describing the nature of the secondary imagination.

A close study of Locke's *Essay* really reveals that Crane has not done justice to him. He attributes to Locke ideas of which Locke cannot be held responsible. But the importance of Crane's essay lies in the fact that it revives Locke, renews our interest in him, and offers a fresh look to Locke's *Essay.* Even the historical interpretation which Crane offers only reinforces Locke's philosophy of the mind: the finite mind has an infinite capacity for thought.

VI

"INTERPRETATION OF TEXTS AND THE HISTORY OF IDEAS"

In the essay "Interpretation of Texts and the History of Ideas" Crane fails to fulfil our expectation. His professed aim in this essay is to indicate the main difficulties in the way of constructing a history of ideas as well as to 'look for solutions of them.' But even after analysing the difficulties and their possible solutions he admits before he ends the essay: "We are back then where we started, with our original difficulties unsolved, or solved only in incomplete and somewhat less than satisfactory ways" (Crane "Interpretation of Texts" 764).

Crane observes that the primary task of the historian of ideas, like any historian, is twofold. First, he must be able to adequately interpret the texts of different varieties—essays, poems, speeches, histories, dialogues, philosophical and scientific treatises, and others—all of which contain ideas and serve as the primary materials of the history of ideas. Second, he must form and execute his own principles of historical construction in order to give integrity to his narrative, without which his book is destined to be a mere 'collection of detached analyses' but not a history proper.

Crane draws our attention to some practical difficulties in connection with the interpretation of texts. Ideas are prevalent in various forms in almost all the branches of knowledge—philosophy, theology, natural science, morality, politics, economics, psychology etc. So the historian of ideas is required to interpret and realize the ideas occurring in those subjects. Here it must be remembered that the same idea may and does occur differently in different subjects. In other words, the writers of different subjects exploit ideas in different ways in keeping with the different principles of construction of their individual subjects. The historian of form must be able to understand which one is a basic idea and which one is only a variety of some other idea. But no historian of ideas, not even a specialist in literary texts, can really attain technical skill in all these varied subject matters. And even if he succeeds in interpreting them in some way, it is very difficult for him to fit them together in a significant frame of historical reference. The historian of ideas thus faces difficulties both on the part of textual interpretation and on the part of inventing appropriate historical principle.

Crane has suggested two possible ways to avoid the difficulties—one is to follow the method of philological investigation and the other is to adopt dialectical method. He illustrates how these methods may help the historian, but at the same time he admits their limitations. The philological method enables the historian to give special care to the elements of words, but the elements of ideas are not so carefully judged by this method. The dialectical method, on the contrary, can do justice to the ideas prevalent in the varieties of subjects, but its power seems lacking on the part of words. Thus it is not enough to achieve scholarly perfection in these methods to be a good historian of ideas. Crane also admits it when he says that "it is not enough to collect materials exhaustively or even to interpret them in a scholarly way; many can do this, and the results, as we all know, are too often dull and unilluminating in the extreme—collections of quotations from many sources, forced into a semblance of unity by means of borrowed formulae ill-understood: to be a Stephen (Leslie Stephen) or a Lovejoy (A.O. Lovejoy) something more is required, namely inventiveness in securing principles and insight in applying them" (Crane "Interpretation of Texts" 762).

At the concluding part of the essay Crane suggests the possibility of inventing another new method in which the subject matter of investigation will neither be words (as the philologists treat them) nor ideas (as dialectical historians conceive them), but a combination of the two. But Crane does not go into the detail of what this third method is and how the historian of ideas is expected to avoid the difficulties in this new method. Therefore, I must recall what I have said at the beginning of this section, namely, Crane in this essay fails to fulfil our expectation.

7

Practical Criticism and R.S. Crane: Study of Individual Authors (Swift, Fielding, Jane Austen and Hemingway)

Occasions when R.S. Crane devotes a whole article to criticize individual literary works are not many. Swift's *Gulliver's Travels*, Fielding's *Tom Jones*, Jane Austen's *Persuasion* and Hemingway's two short stories, *The Killers* and *The Short Happy Life of Francis Macomber* have been individually treated by him. We may also mention two other of his articles, "Notes on the Organization of Locke's Essays" and "Montesquieu and British Thought: Gibbon, Adam Smith, Burke," where Crane's chief concern is with some particular authors and their works. In all other books and essays Crane is the critic of critics. To Express it in a different language, Crane, in most of his books and articles, is mainly concerned with some fundamental critical problems and he tries to suggest possible solutions to those problems. Scattered remarks on individual literary works are of course used in all these essays and books to illustrate his point and substantiate his views. But if we are to find Crane as a practising critic, if we want to judge his act of criticizing individual works in the light of his own critical theory we must turn our attention to those few articles in particular.

However, Crane's treatments of all these authors and their works are not equally elaborate and complete. For, as we all know, Crane examines only the element of plot in *Tom Jones*, and in his article on *Gulliver's Travels* his chief concern is only with the fourth book of that novel. But in his treatment of the two other authors, Jane Austen and Hemingway, Crane is more comprehensive and complete. In my present chapter I shall try to examine Crane's observation on these four authors, and to show what Crane thinks about the function of a literary critic. I leave out of my account the two other articles ("Notes on the Organization of Locke's *Essays*" and "Montesquieu and British Thought: Gibbon, Adam Smith, Burke") because I have already considered them in the previous chapter.

I

"HOUYHNHNMS, YAHOOS, AND THE HISTORY OF IDEAS"

Crane's essay "Houyhnhnms, Yahoos, and the History of Ideas" may be divided into two parts. In the first part Crane sums up most of the available criticism of the fourth voyage of *Gulliver's Travels,* and criticizes one misapplication of the history of ideas in some of the 20th century critics' interpretation of this part of *Guliver's Travels.* Crane's view on the proper method of criticizing a literary work becomes evident in what he says in this part of his essay. In the other part Crane's own interpretation about what Swift actually intended to do in the final travel of Gulliver has been recorded. Crane here seeks to establish how Swift in the fourth voyage of *Gulliver's Travels* intended to disprove a popular tradition in the history of ideas.

It is needless to mention that the fourth voyage of *Gulliver's Travels* created a turmoil in the world of literary criticism, the source of which was nothing but Swift's peculiarly vexing presentation of the man-like Yahoos as the most filthy, degraded and 'unteachable of brutes,' and his treatment of the horselike Houyhnhnms as 'wholly governed by reason.' The charge of a wholehearted misanthropy on the part of the author, which finds its expression through Gulliver, is no longer in vogue now. It has rather been widely accepted as Miss Kathleen M. Williams his pointed out, that the fourth voyage is the culmination of "Swift's life long attack on the pride of man, especially the pride which convinces him that he can live by the light of unaided reason" (Williams 247). But even though the charge of misanthropy has been discarded on the ground that it was due only to a rash judgment of Swift's intention in the fourth voyage, a few other misconceptions are still in vogue. Crane in the opening part of his essay criticizes one such view of some of the 20th century critics, which intends to explain Swift's intention in the fourth voyage on the basis of a hypothesis drawn from the history of ideas.

The hypothesis which these critics have drawn is that Swift has designed the fourth voyage to represent the traditional and orthodox concept of human nature—the concept that there is an inseparable mixture of good and evil in man. They quite naturally tend to explain the two species of animals—the Houyhnhnms and the Yahoos—as allegorical abstractions of good and evil. Swift, they say, might have in view the two extreme opinions about human nature—one was the sentimental optimism of the Earl of Shaftesbury, a contemporary to Swift, and the other was the sheer pessimism of Hobbes and Mandeville, neither of which was a proper estimation of human nature. Swift intended to disprove these two extremist opinions and to uphold the orthodox view that man possesses a nature neither unmixedly good, nor totally bad but an amalgamation of the two. That is why we find him satirizing both the Yahoos and the Houyhnhnms.

Such an interpretation of Swift's intention in the fourth voyage may appear somewhat convincing at first sight, and the critics who exalt it have drawn arguments in favour of their hypothesis from what they find in the text, in Swift's religious belief and also in the general trends of the age. But Crane opposes to this line of interpretation on the ground that it violates the basic condition of hypothesis making. Crane admits it to be true that several possible hypotheses may be framed as primary tools of interpretation of a literary work. It is also true that some positive evidences can be sought out in support of each of the hypotheses. But the critic's task is to find out and establish the correct one from a number of possible ones. And when there remains the scope of only one hypothesis, out of many, to be correct, mere positive evidences are not enough. The critic must try all possible hypotheses, not by accumulating arguments in favour of them but by pointing out the weaknesses, and endeavouring to discard them, if possible, one by one.

Thus, the most appropriate one, which cannot be discarded in this method, will emerge. Only this process will enable the critic to establish his own hypothesis as fact.

But the hypothesis of the allegory of good and evil, Crane observes, when tested in this way can hardly establish itself as fact. The limitation of this popular method of criticism lies in its failure to see other possible interpretations which may also appear to suit the design of the fourth voyage. These critics took it for granted that this part of the travel was meant to reflect a conflict of the three fundamentally different ideas about man's nature—the orthodox classical Christian dualism, the doctrine of the rationalists and benevolists, and that of the materialists and cynics. And then, turning away their attention from all other possibilities, they have engaged themselves only to gather some confirmatory evidences, judiciously avoiding those which do not fit their hypothesis. What these critics have thus, done is only a misapplication of the history of ideas in literary interpretation. Their method being faulty and incomplete, they have ultimately affirmed the false as true.

However, in the second part of his essay Crane has given his own interpretation of Swift's intention in the fourth book of *Gulliver's Travels*. Crane observes that the logicians of antiquity as well as of our own days have been attributing the gift of rationality on man alone in the animal world. In all the definitions of man which they have given from time to time the assumed superiority of man has always been emphasized. Swift, as Crane has tried to establish, designed the fourth voyage with those age-old definitions of man in his mind. As a satirist he desired to disprove what those definitions have emphasized and thus to give a tremendous shock to his readers' pride over the superiority of man. Swift's famous letters to Pope are there in support of Crane's hypothesis. Swift declared that he had "got materials towards a treatise proving the falsity of that definition *animal rational*," and that his chief aim was "to vex the world rather than divert it" (Crane *Humanities* Vol. II 279). This intention might direct Swift to reverse the animal world of Houyhnhnm land and to attribute rationality to the horse like Houyhnhnms and brutish behaviour to the manlike Yahoos.

This reversal was perhaps the most effective means of vexing the world of intellectuals by giving a shock to their complacence of superiority.

Some historical evidences are also there in support of Crane's hypothesis. In the seventeenth and early eighteenth centuries the old fashioned logical treatises were taught in the universities of England. The "Isagoge" of Porphyry was a popular one among them. Porphyry defined men with the help of some binary divisions, popularly known as Porphyrian tree. At the lowest branch of the tree Porphyry divided 'Animal Corporeal Feeling Substance' into 'Rational' and 'Irrational.' Man is the only rational creature; all others go under the other division. And Porphyry mentioned 'the horse' as a concrete example of the irrational variety. Swift, during his days at Trinity College, must have his acquaintance with Porphyry's treatise. His selection of the 'Houyhnhnms,' and no other animal, as opposed to the man-like Yahoos was due to the influence of Porphyrian logic.

Crane has also mentioned an anonymous poem, "The Logician Refuted," in which the poet refused to accept the definition of man as 'animale rationale,' and challenged the logicians to prove it, if they could. The publication of the poem, sometime after *Gulliver's Travels* is surely an evidence of the fact that the matter haunted intellectuals of the time. It was then quite natural for Swift to take it up and to give it a fine satirical twist.

Crane has thus pointed out what tradition of the history of ideas was actually there in Swift's designing of the fourth voyage. His arguments are convincing enough. One may, however, say that Crane has not connected the earlier parts of the *Travels* with the final one. And unless Crane's hypothesis suits the whole design of the book we cannot accept it as fact. But we may, I think, easily have a meaningful explanation of the fourth book quite in tune with the earlier ones in Crane's way of thinking. In the first part of the *Travels* Swift's satire is directed against human pettiness, in the second part against physical grossness, and in the third it is against various institutions and glamorous programmes of man. These three books may be found to have been arranged in an ascending order of importance and seriousness. All these are meant to create the ground for the final shock in the last part.

II

"THE CONCEPT OF PLOT AND THE PLOT OF *TOM JONES*"

In "The Concept of Plot and the Plot of *Tom Jones*" Crane speaks of a new approach to the concept of plot and examines, as a concrete example, the plot of *Tom Jones*. The new approach Crane speaks of is the formalistic approach. As a formalist Crane gives superiority to 'form' over 'content.' In his concept 'form' is the synthesizing factor that gives 'power' and a particular combination to the 'content' or the material aspects of a literary work. It is, for him, the first principle of artistic construction, and should, therefore, be the first principle of a criticism of the textual properties of a work.

However, Crane examines briefly, before he expresses his own concept of a plot, the nature and critical adequacy of the conception of plot that underlies most of the observations of the critics of the past. And he finds that the definition of plot, as the past critics understood it, is an extremely limited one. In their concept plot is only one of the various elements of a novel such as character, thought and diction. It is, they considered, "the material continuity of the story considered in relation to the general pleasure we take in any fiction when our curiosity about the impending events is aroused, sustained, and then satisfied to a degree or in a manner we could not anticipate" (Crane *Critics* 64). Crane also observes that the greatness and goodness of a plot in this sense depend on the variety of incidents it includes, on how the story evokes suspense and surprise, and also on the success the novelist achieves in executing the resolution at the end as a natural outcome of the happenings at the beginning and at the middle of the novel. The inevitable result of such a narrow definition of plot is that a loose external relation between the plot and other aspects of a novel is only considered. And it is, Crane observes, due to such a narrow definition of plot that most of the critical estimates, say of the plot of *Tom Jones*, have finally turned into some enthusiastic general appreciations.

Crane believes that such a restricted definition of plot can hardly do justice to the analysis of the plot of a novel. He, therefore, elaborates his own idea of the plot of a novel. In his concept "the plot of any novel or drama is the particular temporal synthesis effected by the writer of the elements of action, character and thought that constitute the matter of his invention" (Crane *Critics* 66). The elements of action, character, and thought are taken as causal ingredients, and the structure of a plot, as Crane believes, differs widely as the one or the other of these ingredients is employed as the synthesizing principle. We may thus have plots of action, plots of character, and plots of thought. Most of the classical plots generally are plots of action. This may be the reason, Crane rightly observes, why the elements of incidents receive so much importance in the traditional idea of a plot. Critics have actually reduced the concept of the plot to the single element of action, neglecting the two other equally important aspects of character and thought. However, in Crane's concept all the three elements are synthesized in the plot of a novel or a drama. But these three elements constitute what Crane calls the material aspects of a plot, not the form of it. The formal aspect of a plot is the 'power' which every synthesis of the material aspects (action, character and thought) is necessarily endowed with to affect our emotions and opinions in a particular way. The series of actions, events and thoughts of a novel or a drama arouses in us, when we go through it, certain expectations about what is going to happen. In short, we become emotionally involved with whatever happens in the work, and we respond in the particular way in which the plot (or the 'power' of its form) affects us. What Crane suggests here is that the material aspects of action, character, and thought are designed in a particular way or given a definite artistic shape by means of the form of the plot. And the form of a plot is the final end of the artist—his original intention to affect our emotions and reasons or to make us respond in a particular way. All the outward and inward aspects of a novel or a drama are exploited to achieve this definite end. That is why Crane says that "the plot, considered formally, of any imitative work is, in relation to the work as a whole, not simply a means—a 'framework' or 'mere mechanism'—but rather the final end which everything in the work, if that is to be felt as a whole, must be made, directly or indirectly, to serve" (Crane *Critics* 68). Obviously then, the form of a plot, in the particular sense in which Crane uses the term, must be the first principle of a critic to examine effectively any novel or drama he likes to, because unless and until he discovers the formal end of the plot which is the guiding principle of the work and to which all other aspects of the particular work must conform, he can hardly be expected to analyse anything successfully.

In this way Crane elaborates his idea of the plot of a novel or a drama. He then applies this idea to analyse the plot of *Tom Jones*. His is a formalistic analysis, and, therefore, he seeks first to discover the particular form that gives unity to the plot of *Tom Jones*. And for the purpose of discovering this form (which is also the first principle of the artist) a critic must look beyond the material system of happenings that constitutes the external aspects of the plot, and must consider at least three important aspects: (i) One must consider the moral character of the hero that allows us to expect either for a good or a bad fortune for him at the end. (ii) One must also judge the nature of events which take place in the life of the hero, and in consequence of which we expect, whether temporarily or permanently, either a painful or a pleasurable result. (iii) A third important aspect is our idea of the hero's responsibility for whatever happens to him and whatever he does in the novel. Crane emphasizes these three aspects because he thinks that the form of a plot is "a function of the particular correlation among these three variables which the completed work calculated to establish, consistently and progressively, in our minds" (Crane *Critics* 78). And after considering all these aspects in *Tom Jones* Crane discovers that the novel has a 'pervasively comic form.' He supports his idea about this form of the novel with concrete examples from what the text of the novel actually shows.

The happenings of the novel, Crane admits, generate enough suffering for the hero and the heroine of the novel, Tom and Sophia. We sometimes involve ourselves into the distresses of

Tom and wish him to come out of his troubles. All these have a seemingly serious nature. But their sufferings never appear so serious as to arouse the tragic emotions of pity and fear. Crane's impression is that the comic form of the novel prevents the suffering of the hero and the heroine from becoming the dominant emotion in the complication of *Tom Jones.* It prevents even our indignation for the villain from becoming too acute. Fielding has, Crane observes, achieved an attenuation of the serious feelings of pity, fear and indignation—an attenuation which is a necessary condition for comic pleasure—chiefly by two things.

The first thing that Fielding does for this purpose is to endow with certain obvious comic traits those characters in the novel who threaten serious consequences for the hero and the heroine. Blifil is, of course, too selfish to strike us as ridiculous. But some other characters like Allworthy, Lady Bellaston, Lord Fellamar and the Westerns obliviously show some comic strain. And when, Crane observes, the agents of harm are ridiculous persons, we do not generally accept their power of causing harm as well as the matters that follow as a result of their workings so seriously as they appear. The second important thing is that the successive incidents of the novel, as they lead us to the climactic situations, on the one hand increases the suffering of Tom, but on the other hand they make an attentive reader aware of the fact that since nothing irreparable has taken place so far, no such incident is likely to happen in the life of the hero. Such an awareness also reduces the seriousness of actions.

These two things have given a sense of security to the comic pleasure of the novel. Crane has also showed, and convincingly, that the mistaken acts which Tom has committed excite our amusement. Thus the major incidents and characters have been exploited by the novelist for a comic effect. Of course the comic pleasure here is not an unmixed one. It is rather a mixed type of comedy in which all the previous semi-serious happenings end in the happy denouement with a pure rejoicing smile. This, Crane thinks, is the essential form of the novel.

So the primary task of a critic investigating into the novel is, in Crane's opinion, to find out the "extent to which Fielding's handling of the constituent parts of the novel is calculated to sustain and maximize this special pleasure which is its form" (Crane *Critics* 84). Both the merits and demerits of the novel may thus be pointed out. Crane also analyses the novel in this particular way and finds that the novel is not, since no work of art is perhaps perfect, without its faults. We are, for example, not prepared to accept the sudden change in the character of Tom when he borrows money from Lady Bellaston at his very first meeting with her. Similarly the authorial intrusion is often without sufficient artistic justification.

But in spite of some such defects of the novel Crane's impression is that "there are not many novels of comparable length in which the various parts are conceived and developed with a shrewder eye to what is required for a maximum realization of the form" (Crane *Critics* 85). The first thing that Crane mentions in support of what he says is Fielding's skilful handling of the various incidents which directly arise out of Tom's mistakes. Crane shows that Fielding has followed more or less the same pattern for all of them, and the pattern he uses enhances the comic pleasure of the novel. Similarly Feelding's creation of the characters of the novel is quite in tune with the comic form of its plot. Crane also shows how Fielding has even made a full use of the various devices of the mode of narration to help the comic plot form of the novel.

Thus Crane mentions some of the things which must be considered in an analysis of the plot of *Tom Jones*, taken as the first principle of artistic construction. And he suggests that an adequate analysis of the plot of *Tom Jones* in this method will require an examination of how all the major and minor aspects of the novel—characters, dialogues, diction, images and symbols, and even the passages of extra-dramatic thought which define the moral quality of the world—function to hold our responses restricted to the comic form of the novel. Thus this mode of criticism enables us to expose how all the parts of a literary work contribute to achieve the formal end of the artist.

It is, however, a fact that every critical method has its characteristic limitations. Naturally, the formal approach to the plot of a novel, which Crane propounds, may also have some faults. But Crane's greatness lies in the fact that unlike most other critics he is not blind to the defects of his own theory. He is well aware of the limitations of this approach. He, therefore, clearly suggests that this method, even when it can adequately exhibit how the material parts of a work contribute to the achievement of the expected effect, can hardly do justice to the analysis of how the various parts in a work develop themselves. Crane is also aware of the fact that this method is applicable more to evaluate the performance of a writer—his success or failure in constructing individual works of art—than to make a comparative judgment of the literary greatness and seriousness of a work. We will need a method other than the criticism of form to remark, for example, on the general qualities of intelligence and feeling, reflected in *Tom Jones*. Another characteristic fault of this method is that it isolates a work of art as a finished product from the rest of its species. Thus, the method can hardly provide us with a means to judge the place or the relative greatness of a literary work in the history of that type of writings. Crane clearly says that "we have obviously to go beyond formal criticism if we would assess Fielding's originality as a writer of comic romance, or account for that peculiarly eighteenth century flavour in *Tom Jones* which causes us to reflect that, unique and unrepresentative as Fielding's novel is when considered as a whole, it could yet have been written at no other time" (Crane *Critics* 92).

However, this inadequacy of the formal criticism does not affect its positive qualities. What is actually required for the best result is that this method should be supplemented by some other criticism—the criticism of quality and also some sorts of historical inquiries. But the theory must be valued as the only effective method that can adequately analyse, in terms of causes and effects rather than analogies, the values and characteristics of a literary work as an artistic construction with a special power to affect us in a particular way. Crane suggests one more point, though he does not elaborate it. His suggestion is that the investigation into the historical origins of a work, as well as the criticism of qualities become more specific and reliable when they are controlled by the criticism of form. There is surely sense in what Crane suggests here. Any criticism—whether historical or psychological—must be supported by what the literary text as the only concrete object bears testimony to. A criticism of form can almost faultlessly exhibit what the artist tries to achieve in a given work of art. Naturally, when all other criticisms are based on the criticism of form, they may give us more accurate information about their investigations. To add one more point, the idea of 'form' which Crane expresses here is expressed more elaborately toward the end of his book *The Languages of Criticism and the Structure of Poetry*. In that book Crane applies his idea of form in the analysis of the structure of poetry. It proves that Crane's idea of 'form' is basically the same. It is constituted as a theory applicable perhaps to all types of literary works of true artistic value.

III

"JANE AUSTEN: *PERSUASION*"

Crane's consideration of Jane Austen's *Persuasion*, as has already been said, is more comprehensive and elaborate than that of either Swift or Fielding. The essential story of *Persuasion*, Crane observes, is the story of "a broken engagement finally restored, and with even deeper happiness for the heroine and hero, Anne Elliot and Captain Frederick Wentworth, than they had felt when the engagement was entered into eight years and a half before" (Crane *Humanities* Vol. II 283). The story is a simple one and Jane Austen has presented it simply by means of a large number of characters and a series of often disconnected events. Apparently, for a simple story that Jane Austen tells in *Persuasion* such a huge number of characters and events seem superfluous. Crane, therefore, frames his critical questions from this point. He tries to investigate what all the minor characters and series of events do in relation to the main story of the novel. He also tries to find out Jane Austen's artistic problems and their solutions from the artists' point of view.

Persuasion, as Crane understands it, is a love story of a different character. It is a love story indeed, and a simple one in the sense that there is hardly any external obstacle working as a bar to the delayed union of the lovers. It is more than an ordinary love story, primarily because a love story of common character depends for its appeal and emotional strength chiefly on our general sympathy with young lovers. But Jane Austen has conceived her novel in a bit different way in order to evoke a different kind of response at the climax. In support of his belief Crane mentions the paragraph in which the narrator (Jane Austen) informs us how Anne and Wentworth exchanged their feelings and pleasures immediately after Charles had taken leave of them. Crane believes that the response of the reader at this point of the novel is more than mere sympathy with the lovers. We, the readers, share the 'rational' and 'rapturous' happiness of Anne and Wentworth. It is the happiness "not simply of lovers but of *moral individualists*—a happiness which can be achieved only by persons of superior minds and characters, and to which, consequently, when we are convinced that this is indeed the case, we tend to respond in a more complex way than to the merely 'sentimental' resolutions of ordinary love tales" (Crane *Humanities* Vol. II 288-89).

In order to evoke such a response Jane Austen had to mould her materials differently. Crane observes that she might begin her story at the very beginning when Anne and Wentworth were first engaged. She might even contrive her narrative in a way that we were allowed to enter into the thoughts of Wentworth also. But in either case she might not be able to arouse the desired response. That is why Austen follows neither of these forms. She makes Anne the centre of her narrative, and "except in the opening exposition and in a relatively few scattered passages later on we are given no more of the events and of the thoughts of the other characters than Anne herself can know through direct observation and listening to conversations or through not always correct inference from what she sees or hears" (Crane *Humanities* Vol. II 289). The narrative follows her wherever she goes.

This very design of the novel, Crane shows, necessitates the inclusion of a large number of characters and events. The ultimate union of Anne and Wentworth, as already mentioned, is something more than a union of two lovers—it is the union of two good minds, two *moral* individuals. That is why the happiness is greater than what might have been when they first met. But if readers are to share this feeling of greater happiness, they must be convinced of the moral and constant characters of the hero and the heroine. But the design of the novel is such that the hero and the heroine are not given the scope of a joint response until at the end. Naturally, the novelist had to expose their minds through their interactions with other characters and responses to various activities and events in their day-to-day lives. Hence, Austen had to introduce a large number of minor characters and events. If they are removed, it would be well-nigh impossible to have the desired effect. In short, it is the form of the novel that determines the materials.

After examining the novelist's intention, and its relation to the design of the novel, Crane tries to judge the artistic problems of the novelist and the manner in which she solves them. The development of the plot of *Persuasion* is the development or changes in the mental world of Anne and Wentworth. So Jane Austen had to face the problem of invention and treatment in order to unfold the minds of the hero and the heroine and to make the reunion convincing. She had to invent such incidents, or 'occasions' as Crane calls them, which would successfully give expression to the gradual development of the plot, and at the same time had to give variety and probability to those incidents. Any conscious reader, who goes through the novel, must admit that Jane Austen has successfully solved these problems.

A number of critics have brought the charge against the novelist of *Persuasion* of using a series of coincidences which, according to them, hardly suit the practice of a good artist. Crane comes forward to vindicate Jane Austen's practice. Crane admits that Austen has taken help of coincidences to make possible the meeting between Anne and Wentworth. But the fact is that the artistic quality of the novel is not hampered even a bit by them. The force of the novel does not allow us to consider them as coincidences. Even if we, for the sake of criticism, admit that they are coincidences, we must also admit that Jane Austen had no alternative before her. The mental conditions of the hero and the heroine are such that they cannot invite one another, and naturally their meeting is possible only by chances and coincidences.

Crane also observes that a novel like *Persuasion* depends for its success on the readers' wholehearted attachment to the heroine, Anne, as an individual, because the more we feel for her the more we understand what happens. We gradually become eager to find her happy, and when we find that our expectation is fulfilled at last we enjoy boundless pleasure. So Jane Austen's problem was to build Anne's character in that way. And Crane shows that the novelist has followed three principal devices for the desired result.

First, Jane Austen handles quite skilfully Anne's unspoken thought in the narrator's discourse. In some short passages the narrator expresses the suppressed mental suffering of the heroine. These analytical passages are quite functional; they help to draw the readers' sympathy for Anne. Second, the novelist tries to invent such happenings and conversations that "define and vivify for us her (Anne's) positive traits of personality and character: her serious principles, her superior standards, her sound judgments of people, her ability to look at herself and others (including Wentworth) objectively" (Crane *Humanities* Vol. II 296). The more we know such good qualities of the heroine the more we become emotionally attached to her. A third main device followed by Austen is to juxtapose Anne with other characters of the novel, which also enable us to recognise her goodness as well as greatness. Anne feels her emotional proximity to the characters like Admiral and Mrs. Croft and the Hervilles, who impress us as pleasant, warm-hearted, self-reliant and unpretentious. This likeness of feeling and opinion makes Anne impressive to the readers. Thus, Jane Austen solves the problem of building Anne's character.

In the creation of the character of Wentworth also Jane Austen has achieved enormous success. Crane considers Wentworth as one of the greatest heroes of Jane Austen. Austen had to make him superior in nature so that Anne finds some renewed attraction for him. And the novelist has established her hero's superiority in various artistic ways, without any direct comment. Various activities and incidents in the novel throw light on the goodness of Wentworth's character. Besides, when we contrast Wentworth with other characters like Walter Elliot, Charles Musgrove and Mrs. Elliot, we can easily discern his superiority. Again, Wentworth's closest friends are those whom Anne regards to be the warm-hearted and ideal people. It is also another proof of Wentworth's warm-heartedness and sincerity. Thus, the problem of building the character of Wentworth is also solved.

It is in this way that Crane criticises the novel. There is no conflict between theory and practice in Crane: he follows what he says. He examines and explains the textual and artistic problems without imposing any dogmatic principle. His criticism is, again, positive in nature. Unlike most other critics who burden their criticisms with what the artist has failed to achieve, Crane shows us convincingly what Jane Austen as an artist has achieved and how. His observations are thus more helpful for a better understanding of the text.

Crane's essay on *Persuasion* is also interesting for the reason that here he emerges as a moral critic. Apart from the consideration of the plot structure and the principles evolved from within, Crane spent a good deal of energy in highlighting the moral thrust of the novel by pointing out, time and again, the moral quality of the love between Anne and Wentworth. The union after the restoration of the relationship is qualitatively better than the possible union in the beginning of their relationship, because both the characters have known each other better during the intervening period and each appreciates the moral qualities of the other. By the end of the novel, Crane suggests, their love is touched by mutual admiration in addition to attraction which they felt at the outset for each other.

IV

"EARNEST HEMINGWAY: *THE KILLERS*"

Crane has written two articles on two different stories of Hemingway. It is interesting to note that both the articles are in the form of letters written as responses to the observations of a friend and an ex-student. In his article on "The Killers" Crane concentrates his attention on the "technical question of how the characters, actions, and speeches of the boys in the lunch room are related to the situation involving the killers and Ole Andreson" (Crane *Humanities* Vol. II 303). With regard to this consideration Crane divides the characters of "The Killers" into two groups—one belonging to the 'subject' of the story and the other to the 'treatment.' His distinction between 'subject' and 'treatment,' Crane admits, is in the sense of what Henry James in his preface to *The Portrait of a Lady* says about that distinction. The subject proper of "The Killers" is comprised of just three characters—Ole Andreson and the two killers, Al and Max. All the remaining characters, according to Crane, are related to the subject only indirectly. They belong intimately to the 'treatment' because they are used as "devices of disclosure and commentary which enable Hemingway to bring his essential 'subject' before us with a maximum of concentration and dramatic liveliness and a minimum of ambiguity as to its desired emotional effect" (Crane *Humanities* Vol. II 304). Crane tries to prove this point with sufficient examples and illustrations from the text. Firstly, the essence of the story is constituted of the fact that the killers, Al and Max, are bent on murdering Ole, and they are going to succeed simply because Ole, in spite of being aware of it, decides to do nothing to escape. The happenings in the lunch room and the activities of Nick and his friends by no means affect or change this essence of the story and its expected development.

Secondly, the peculiar moral and emotional response arising out of the action of the story is, Crane suggests, due to the horrifying quality of the killers and also to Ole's passive submission to his fate. Our emotional response to the story is what George and Nick, respectively, say: "It's a hell of a thing," and "It's an awful thing" (Hemingway 264).

The boys in the lunch room have no contribution in creating that response; their activities only clarify for the readers the desired response. The artist, Crane suggests, could invent any other situation as well to give expression to his essential subject and to create the same emotional response. In support of his idea Crane mentions Hemingway's deliberate vagueness about

Ole's offence. Al and Max, we are informed in the text, are going to kill Ole only to oblige a friend. And Ole informs us that he has got in wrong. But the exact nature of his offence is kept secret. This is, Crane says, part of Hemingway's design to "shift the main emphasis of the story away from causes and antecedents to the final situation resulting from these [...] the horrifying quality of the two killers and their completely impersonal relation to Ole, and the even more 'awful' quality of Ole's passive acquiescence in his fate" (Crane *Humanities* Vol. II 307).

In this way Crane shows that the boys in the lunch room have almost nothing to do either as constituents of action or as agents to produce the ultimate effect. But at the same time Crane admits that their artistic function in the story is enormous. He divides the story into four scenes and shows how George, Nick and Sam are made to function in the action of the story. In the first scene the two killers are the centre of attention, but here Hemingway has utilized George to the full for the purpose of giving us all the necessary information. The second brief scene is the preparatory part of our meeting Ole Andreson. Here Nick's willingness to go to Ole as a messenger makes a smooth development of the plot possible. It does not, however, change or modify the plot. The third scene is again like the first one a scene of disclosure, and Nick's role here is almost the same as the role of George in the first scene. Nick's message had nothing new for Ole, and neither Nick nor his message brings about any change in the imminent action of the story. The final scene, by means of the reactions of George and Nick, suggests the possible reaction of the readers. The function they serve here is more or less the function of a chorus. Thus, Crane shows that the second group of characters is part of Hemingway's artistic treatment.

Crane also opposes the view of Brooks and Warren, who consider Nick Adams to be the central character of the story. The story, according to them, is the development of Nick from adolescence to manhood by means of the shocking experiences he passes through. Crane rejects this theory on two grounds. His first point is that there is no development from adolescence to manhood in the character of Nick. He simply passes from ignorance to knowledge. Crane's second objection is that the character of Nick impresses us by no means as the central character of the story. The attention of the readers is never centralized on him. So, Crane's impression is that the story is most meaningfully illustrated when we think of the boys in the lunch room as 'utility' characters. "Each boy," Crane observes, "has his own special job to do in disclosing to us Hemingway's 'subject' in its two essential aspects: George to help us understand and feel the killers, Nick to give us Ole" (Crane *Humanities* Vol. II 313). This observation of Crane is so logical and closely related to the textual properties of the story that we can hardly think of an alternative explanation.

Crane's essay on "The Killers" is particularly interesting because Crane starts with a basic premise laid down by the master of modern fiction, Henry James. Placing the story neatly within the framework laid down by James, Crane proceeds to examine "The Killers" in terms of Aristotelian notion of Plot. This is quite justified because "The Killers," though a short story, is full of dramatic elements. The entire story is constituted of a string of conversations connected by a very thin ribbon of commentary. Secondly, the story is dominated by action, ending with a definite suggestion of Ole's imminent death.

As a formalist Crane has taken into account the emotional form of the story and shows how the vagueness of Ole's offence contributes to the richness of the story. Crane's analysis of the story also shows his remarkable ability to handle short story—a genre not known to Aristotle—in Aristotelian terms. The essay seems to suggest that any creative, cognitive discourse is amenable to analysis by Aristotelian criteria. The study is highly original, very profound and full of critical insights.

V

"EARNEST HEMINGWAY: *THE SHORT HAPPY LIFE OF FRANCIS MACOMBER*"

In the essay on "The Short Happy Life of Francis Macomber" also, as in the article on "The Killers," Crane applies the Aristotelian canons in order to ascertain the nature of Macomber's tragedy. In order to do this he discusses in detail the essential nature of an Aristotelian tragedy arising out of (i) the formal cause, (ii) the material cause and (iii) the efficient cause. In the process he also takes up the Aristotelian notion of Catharsis. Crane makes a fine anatomy of the story in great detail and depth, and shows how the story fails to fulfil the Aristotelian criteria of tragedy. Crane, however, does not impose anything on the story form outside (*ab extra*), but elicits the information from inside (*ab intra*) to show how the plot is developed. A true Aristotelian he starts with an analysis of the (desired) effect on the readers and retrospectively identifies the factors that contribute to this effect.

Crane shows that the plot form of "The Short Happy Life of Francis Macomber" is different from the plot of tragedy as defined by Aristotle. A tragic plot, roughly speaking, requires the change of fortune from good to bad, and the ultimate effect of such a plot is a catharsis of pity and fear. But in this story, Crane rightly says, "The change upon which the effect depends is not a change of fortune from good to bad but of character from bad to good" (Crane *Humanities* Vol. II 319). For, Macomber starts in his lowest condition (in the lion hunting) and proceeds to his greatest achievement before death. He has risen from the depth of unhappiness. His course of action and death, unlike that of a tragic hero, is not caused by 'hamartia.' The only similarity of the story with a tragedy in Aristotelian sense is that it involves the issues of life and death. But even then "they are involved in such a way that we do not experience fear for Macomber as he proceeds to assert his new-found courage or pity for him when he falls" (Crane *Humanities* Vol. II 319). Naturally, the position of an Aristotelian tragic hero can hardly be claimed for Macomber.

Crane shows that Macomber-like characters (Cuckolds in subjection to their wives) have a long literary tradition. At first they were mere comic butts. But in the twentieth century such characters are often found as protagonists in serious plots. They are found to act unexpectedly and to create thus an impression of nobility. Crane believes that Hemingway in this story has done the same thing.

However, in respect of its construction Crane does not

consider this story as one of the best stories of Hemingway. He observes that the plot of this story, unlike the plots of some of the best short stories, is too obvious. Macomber starts as an abject coward. He appears as a slave to Margot. Naturally, the only expected development of his character is to get over his fear as well as to make himself free from his wife's subjection. Crane also finds that Hemingway has taken resort to some easier devices in presenting his story. The opening part of the story, he says, arouses the expectation of "an objective and dramatic rendering of events in the manner, for instance, of 'The killers'" (Crane *Humanities* Vol. II 324). But gradually the author changes his device and Wilson is found to act as an observer-chorus. And towards the end of the story Hemingway takes help of direct statements of thought and feeling for both Macomber and Margot.

All of us, I think, will agree with Crane that Macomber is not a tragic hero in the Aristotelian sense. We may also agree with him in respect of what he says about the construction of the story, but it is difficult to agree with him that Margot deliberately killed Macomber out of hatred. A close reading of the concluding section of the story would lead us to different conclusion. In the beginning of the story Margot has definite hatred for Macomber. In fact, she even spites him by kissing Wilson in his presence. Before the buffalo hunt Wilson and Margot gravitate towards each other, although it is made abundantly clear that Wilson is a strong man and Margot goes to him mainly because she cannot stand her husband's cowardice. The buffalo hunt turns the whole situation upside down. For the first time Margot sees how Macomber can rise above his cowardice, behave courageously and face a charging buffalo. It is only then that sitting alone in the car Margot underwent a change and her ideas about her husband also changed. This is precisely the reason why at the last moment when she thinks that Macomber is about to be overpowered by the buffalo she tries to shoot it, but accidentally the bullet hits her husband and kills him. It *is* an accident. Otherwise she would not sit crying in the corner when Wilson comes to congratulate her: "Then he walked over to the motor car where the woman sat crying in the corner. 'That was a pretty thing to do,' he said in a toneless voice. 'He *would* have left you too.' 'Stop it,' she said" (Hemingway 42). The crying of Margot, her resistance to Wilson, her inability to feel elated over her husband's death clearly indicate that she had no intention to murder her husband, in which case she would have felt happy in succeeding in her mission and getting rid of an impediment in her union with Wilson. But that does not happen. In the course of the last twenty lines she uses the words "stop it" eight times. This shows the crowded emotions, the confused state of mind which can be explained only if we take Macomber's death as an accident. Wilson, a professional hunter, is a man of low perceptivity and therefore cannot understand the complex of feelings which Margot experiences.

VI

Crane believes that literary work should primarily be judged by principles evolved from within the text. The critic without being led dogmatically by the principles of any particular *-ism*, should try to explore the actual intention of the author. He should pay adequate attention to the artistic and structural problems faced by the author, and try to judge how far and by what means the author solves his problems. Crane's performance in the essays analysed in this chapter is quite in keeping with this idea of the function of a literary critic. In each of the essays, as we have seen, Crane has tried to discover the distinctive problems (artistic and structural) of each of the authors in their actual act of creation, and on the basis of his observation he suggests how far they have succeeded in solving their individual problems. And what is remarkable in his observation is that he does not impose any critical theory from outside in any of his discussion. While most of the critics approach a literary text with a particular theory in mind and analyse the text as the theory directs or allows them to do, in Crane's method the textual properties of a work—what the author actually does in it—exhibit the theoretical aspects, if any, attached to that work. His primary concern is with what the text, as the concrete literary object, actually contains. Thus in his analysis of the fourth voyage of *Gulliver's Travels* as well as of *Tom Jones* he contradicts some existing or established ideas, and confirms his own opinions on the basis of a detailed analysis of all the possible sides of the texts.

Another important quality of Crane as a practising critic is that unlike most other critics who speak more about what the artist fails to achieve, he is chiefly engaged in what (and how) the artist does achieve in his work. Thus, his way of criticism surely helps us to increase our knowledge of the text through its proper understanding.

Above everything else, however, we must note Crane's true wisdom and liberal mindedness as a literary critic. He is never dogmatic. He admits the limitations of a literary theory—its incapability of judging all types of literary works quite effectively and well. That is why he suggests, in his analysis of *Tom Jones*, that for the best result formal criticism should accompany historical criticism also. This attitude is something uncommon (but surely welcome) in practical criticism. For Crane, however, this practice is quite natural because it is part of Crane's pluralistic attitude.

8

Some Other Critical Essays

Some other articles or critical observations which have not been discussed so for in this book also testify Crane's achievement as a literary critic. In this chapter I intend to analyse some such articles of R.S. Crane. Crane's observations in these articles, in my view, are still valid to a great extent. These include (i) "Criticism as Inquiry; or The Perils of the 'High Priori Road,'" (ii) "On Hypotheses in 'Historical criticism': Apropos of Certain Contemporary Medievalists," (iii) "History Versus Criticism in the Study of Literature," (iv) "Varieties of Dramatic Criticism" and (v) "Every Man His Own Critic."

I

"CRITICISM AS INQUIRY; OR, THE PERILS OF THE 'HIGH PRIORI ROAD'"

In "Criticism as Inquiry; or, The Perils of the 'High Priori Road,'" Crane criticises the New Criticism which brought about a revolutionary change in the field of literary study, replacing the traditional form of historical scholarship. His criticism, however, is not directed against the formation of the New Critical theory of literary study because Crane, as a pluralist, knows that the emergence of new theories is a historical inevitability and also because he believes that each of the critical theories, if properly utilized, may contribute something towards our understanding, enjoyment and evaluation of literary works. He, in fact, expresses his concern over the "emergence within criticism itself of modes of thinking about literature which make not merely for a separation in practice between critical discussion and historical scholarship, but for a sharp and irreconcilable opposition in principle between the two fields" (Crane *Humanities* Vol. II 27). Crane in this article shows, and convincingly, that for the New Criticism a literary work is a closed system of empirical data. What he objects to is that the New Critics have certain paranoiac ideas such as "the unifying significance of a poetic drama is normally given by its patterns of recurrent imagery; the belief that literary structure is typically a matter of ironical tension" (Crane *Humanities* Vol. II 43) etc. which predetermine their judgment. The point that Crane tries to make is that in spite of their protestations for objective criticism the New Critics are basically subjective in their approach. They fail to come out of the grip of New Criticism. Consequently many important aspects are lost sight of.

In the trial period of criticism during the thirties—when it was struggling to achieve a popular and respectable place—it was perhaps more or less justified to set it in an antithetical balance to historical scholarship. One can understand, possibly appreciate, the activities of the critics then to minimise the importance of the problems with which the historical scholars mainly concern themselves and to maximise the values of critical study. But the indifference of these critics in bridging the gap between criticism and historical-philosophical scholarship cannot be supported. Crane's opinion is that when criticism overcomes its crisis and establishes itself as a popular branch of studying literary art one should try to remove the misconception regarding the relationship between criticism and historical scholarship. For actually there is hardly any contradiction between them; they are in fact complementary to each other. It is, then, the duty of the friends of criticism to reconstruct the university studies. The philological-historical tradition is required to be carried on and reinvigorated, developing at the same time "what that tradition had been relatively weak in—systematic training in the various modes of critical analysis and judgment" (Crane *Humanities* Vol. II 27). It is really not proper to subvert the older order of teaching and research; it is harmful even to criticism. The critics of the thirties, most of them, failed to realize it. They were blind to the fact that as the historical order of study remains incomplete without critical analysis and judgment, similarly "there can be no adequate criticism that is not solidly based on the history of the art with which it is concerned" (Crane *Humanities* Vol. II 27).

After pointing out this primary fault of the New Critics Crane takes up his major concern in the essay—the limitations of their critical practice. Criticism is some sort of inquiry and the findings of critical inquiry are expected to be harmonious to a great degree to what the writer has achieved in the text—the richness of imagination, subtlety of implications, emotional powers etc. Otherwise the critical findings will merely be some isolated impressions of the critic, not criticism proper. In other words, the critical findings must be well grounded on the concrete evidences from inside and outside the text. The New Critics are often found to miss this point.

In this context Crane informs us that a good critic when he approaches to judge a piece of literary work should have a few things in mind:

(a) The critic is required to have "a habitual distrust of the *a priori*."

(b) He must take help of theories as needed but should remember all the time that any theory, used to evaluate human activities, is inevitably incomplete because new elements are always expected to appear with every new creation. Theories, even the most up to date ones are therefore inadequate to explain and evaluate the newer elements of art.

(c) He should also remember that there is no necessary connection between the grounds on which he employs a working hypothesis and the grounds on which it is confirmed. He must keep a suspicious eye on the ruling hypothesis. The confirmation of a hypothesis can only be achieved when the probability of the hypothesis can be weighed (with a mind as free as possible from doctrinal prepossessions) against the probabilities of all other relevant hypotheses that he can think of. It may be mentioned here that Crane has elaborated his views on hypothesis in the essay "On Hypothesis in Historical Criticism."

The New Critics, Crane claims, in their uses of hypotheses as well as in their method of critical investigation are faulty. They reacted against historical scholarship but failed to substitute it by an all encompassing fruitful and perfect method to judge literary art. That is why Crane complains that "in relation to the best standards of factual inquiry and proof recognised in other humanistic fields, the general tendency of the movement has been reactionary and obscurantist. This appears both in the kind of theorising about literature it has encouraged and in its characteristic procedures in practical criticism" (Crane *Humanities* Vol. II 31). Let us now see how Crane justifies his point.

One popular practice of the New Critics is "to reduce to a single formula the overwhelming variety of aims, subjects, moods, views of life, forms, methods, uses of language he has encountered in past and present writings which have gone under the names of 'literature' or 'poetry'" (Crane *Humanities* Vol. II 32). It is thus that we find propositions like "the language of poetry is the language of paradox" or "literature is ultimately metaphorical and symbolic." As first principles these critics suddenly take up such propositions which apparently have a universal or semi-universal scope of application and then come down to explain the literary texts in the light of those principles. Another way of establishing first principles followed by these critics is "essentially a method of dialectical analysis in which you begin by laying down some general postulate—as for example that poetry is the polar opposite of science and then proceed to work out logically all the implications of this" (Crane *Humanities* Vol. II 33). This method is more or less the same as the old method of bipartite division.

Now, this method of explaining the inner properties of a piece of literary work, poetry for example, is according to Crane, inappropriate because it is not properly applicable to literature and secondly because it is incompatible with the mode of inquiry which is essential to criticism. Crane mentions two major reasons why this method is inappropriate:

(a) Literature is not something natural but human creation—art. And like any other art dealing with man and the world an interaction between man and the world is infinitely complex so that each word in spite of some generic homogeneity is unique mode of discourse. No common criteria—however refined—can be adequate to cover the universe of discourse contained within a literary work. In other words the New Critics suffer from the fallacy of hasty generalization in regard to literary works. Crane offers this argument as much to point out the natural deficiency of the New Critics as to make the claims of pluralistic criticism obvious. These critics tend to reduce literary art to a single set of principles, but literature is not liable to such reduction. There is nothing predetermined in literature. "To attempt therefore to derive its nature *a priori* from general postulates, to geometrize about it—for that is what these theorists in effect have been doing—is wholly to miss the point" (Crane *Humanities* Vol. II 36).

(b) The method of dialectical analysis through contrasts which these critics employ can never determine the actually operative principles of construction, meaning or value in literature. If, for example, we do a contrastive study of a poem and a scientific treatise, the point we miss is that the two are different types of production and therefore require two different modes to analyse and judge their inner characters.

Crane reaffirms that the practice of the New Critics is incompatible with the mode of enquiry in the sense that the enquiry is more or less predetermined. They simply find in literary work what they want to find and are completely blind to many important aspects because of their monistic approach. The peculiar elements which do not come under the principles remain unobserved. All theorizings of this kind actually reduce inquiry into a "mere application of pre-established dogmas" and the critic cannot discover anything beyond what is already known. The problem arises out of the fact that the New Critics insulated from history ignored the most vital fact that a literary work does not exist in vacuum. It is produced at a particular point of time in history and is, therefore, governed by all the historical forces operating at that particular point of time. To ignore this fact is to decontextualize a literary work, which is bound to result in a criticism that loses touch with reality. The result naturally is pre-determined by the dogmas. There is no scope of a fresh discovery in this type of critical research.

This faulty approach to literature is called the 'dialectical fallacy' by R.S. Crane. He shows that it is often possible to discover a meaning of a literary work as one desires and thus one can show the applicability of his theory. But what one fails to see here is that any other critic may in the same way fit his own theory to the same work. This is what happens in case of these critics. Every one of them takes it for granted that his hypothesis is quite in tune with the work he judges, and therefore feels no urge to justify the applicability of his hypothesis against other possible ones. He hardly feels the necessity to support his findings with sufficient documentary evidences. In *The Burning Fountain* Wheelwright, for example, discovers 'plurisignation' in his explanation of Marvell's couplet. There may actually remain 'plurisignation' in the poem but why should we think in the way Wheelwright wants us to think? The point is that Wheelwright should have argued the case and established his point with sufficient proofs from both inside and outside the text, if necessary, so that we are convinced of the presence of plurisignation against other possibilities.

Thus, Crane shows how the New Critics fail to offer us an organized form of criticism, though they may claim credit enough to popularize criticism and to give it a proper place in the academic world. As a result of it criticism has failed to a great extent to come out as a serious branch of learning. Therefore, at the concluding part of the essay Crane suggests a few remedial measures which will, he thinks, help to make criticism really an interesting and serious branch of study. These are as follows:

(i) The students, before they take up the job of a critic should pass through all the rigours as scholars. Otherwise they will be tempted to take up any method without testing it sufficiently.

(ii) They should be encouraged all the time to justify

whatever they say and, in the same way, to explain (not with the help of established theories) how they know something in the text to be true.

(iii) Bad methods in criticism must be rebuked. One will then be serious enough in the field of theorizing.

(iv) A serious endeavour should be made to develop a body of general knowledge of literature, "grounded in literary history and practical experience of writing instead of in dialectic merely" (Crane *Humanities* Vol. II 44).

(v) The teachers in their teaching and practice should try to inculcate on the students "an exploratory and inquiring rather than a doctrinaire use of such knowledge in studies of particular works and writers" (Crane *Humanities* Vol. II 44).

This essay may be regarded as an important addition to the collection of critical writings which point out the defects of New Criticism. It helps Criticism to be more organised. One thing, however, to be noticed here is that Crane does not bring under his consideration some obvious and much discussed defects of the New Critics like their lack of historical sense or banishment of all extra textual considerations from the scope of criticism. He concentrates his attention on the theoretical defects of the New Critics—their deficiency in the selection of first principles and their deviation from proper inquiry. These are actually there behind the New Critics' failure to make criticism a serious branch of study.

Crane's opinion regarding the complementary relation between criticism and historical scholarship is really valuable. One may consider it lightly, saying that Crane's pluralistic attitude is always in search of synthesizing more than one method and principle. But whatever may be said, we can hardly deny the truth of his suggestion that the two should be interdependent for the best result in literary study.

The suggestions Crane gives at the end of the essay are equally important. That Crane is an academician is proved from what he suggests. He considers criticism as a subject to be taught and learnt in the classroom. That is why his suggestions are valuable to both students and teachers. But more importantly the essay is of signal importance because it registers strong reasoned protest against the basic assumptions of New Criticism in its heyday and thus anticipates the reaction against New Criticism that started later in 1967 with the Deconstructionists. The essay is therefore important for both its practical values and its historical significance.

II

"ON HYPOTHESES IN 'HISTORICAL CRITICISM': APROPOS OF CERTAIN CONTEMPORARY MEDIEVALISTS"

R.S. Crane in this essay examines and shows the proper uses and many of the existing misuses of hypotheses primarily in relation to the historical interpretation of literary texts. His method of using hypotheses, he claims, is applicable to other fields of interpretation as well. The stimulus he receives to write this essay is from the publications of D.W. Robertson, Jr. and others of the school of American medievalists who have failed to realize the proper use of hypotheses in the historical interpretation of text. In the opening part of the essay Crane restricts himself to the analysis of hypotheses in general. He examines the various popular ways of how different hypotheses are formed and applied to the interpretation of literary texts and finally suggests the most effective one with enough of positive arguments. In the concluding part of the essay the actual practice of Robertson and others is examined in the light of the theoretical observations made in the earlier part of the essay. In a way of contrast he exhibits the limitation of their observation and method.

The job of interpreting literary texts critically presupposes the act of finding answers to certain questions which we may or do ask about the literary text in hand. In other words, we try to find solutions to certain critical problems. And before we are confirmed of a particular solution, we start with a number of probable hypotheses. Crane calls them particular hypotheses because their reference in only to the literary text in hand. In this act of forming particular hypotheses to a critical problem consists the primary stage of critical interpretation. The next important stage of critical interpretation is that of testing the hypotheses on the basis of the principles and provisions available in the text and of establishing thereby a particular hypothesis as fact. All the confusions and misuses relating to hypotheses take place in this stage of testing the interpretative hypotheses.

Crane has observed that two common assumptions about hypotheses guide, whether consciously or not, the act of critical interpretation. One is that "certain hypotheses, or kinds of hypotheses, contain in themselves, by virtue of their nature or origin and quite apart from the immediate facts of the case, a greater likelihood of proving correct than other hypotheses relative to the same text" (Crane *Humanities* Vol. II 238). This sort of preference or privilege given to some hypotheses, however, is purely on the basis of some general considerations or ideas of an age or literature in general, prior to any critical scrutiny of their applicability to a particular work. Crane calls it "the doctrine of the privileged hypotheses" (Crane *Humanities* Vol. II 238). But the fact remains that this "doctrine of the privileged hypotheses" does not help us in any way to establish our hypotheses as facts. For, literature does not follow any fixed rule or manner. The truth contained in most works of an age may not be the truth of all works of that age. Thus, this doctrine may only help us in discarding the most impossible hypothesis about a work. It may, for example, direct us not to apply the Marxist theory of criticism or artistic construction to any medieval poetry. For, all of us know that this theory was foreign to the poets of that period, and the poets naturally had hardly any scope of constructing their artistic wholes with that theory in mind. The 'doctrine of the privileged hypothesis' can help us only to this far, but no farther.

The other assumption about hypotheses is, as Crane calls it, 'the doctrine on the sufficiency of positive corroboration.' A critic by virtue of this assumption is led to treat a hypothesis as "an already partly established thesis and conceives of the remaining stage in the inquiry as a search for further confirmation of its truth rather than as a critical examination of its claims" (Crane *Humanities* Vol. II 241). The critic looks for only some positive supports of his hypothesis. He selects only those elements of the text which suit his hypothesis, neglecting or avoiding skilfully those others which misfit or even go against the hypothesis. And finally the critic considers his hypothesis to be confirmed as fact if "particulars can be found within the text or outside it which either harmonize with it or can be construed to harmonize with it" (Crane *Humanities* Vol. II 241).

Crane rejects this way of critical investigation and of confirming one's hypothesis. His point is that the character of the literary texts is such that they can contain more than one intention or meaning. It is, therefore, possible to draw positive supportable evidence for more than one hypothesis. We are often offered some widely variant or even contradictory interpretations of a literary text, for each one of which the respective interpreter presents a body of supportable evidence from inside as well as from outside the text. We can hardly be sure of what actually happens in the work. The hypotheses actually remain as hypotheses and are not established as fact. This outcome is enough to prove the falsity of this method of selecting and testing of hypotheses. That is why Crane objects to this method.

Crane's objections in this respect do not really hold water if put under rigorous scrutiny. To start with a hypothesis is only the beginning and not the end of the discovery procedure. Any serious researcher while developing his hypothesis through substantiation, is bound to consider and reject many other possibilities. Crane's objections here is basically theoretical; it cannot be applicable to criticism as really practised.

However, it must be noted that Crane's objection is not to the framing of usable hypotheses but to the conduct of interpretative inquiries required to establish a hypothesis as fact. The aim of a critic in his attempt to examine a literary text should be to discover the *actual* intention of the author, not a probable one. "The ideal is to be able to say—and to say convincingly to both ourselves and other scholars—about any interpretation of a given text, not merely that *if* its author's intention was such-and-such, he might very well have written as he did—that is still only hypothesis—but that *only if* his intention was such-and-such would he in all probability have written as he did" (Crane *Humanities* Vol. II 244). It is of course true that such an ideal is not easy to achieve. Crane also admits it. Still he sets this ideal with the purpose that a maximum perfection towards it will enable the critic to be nearest to the author's actual intention. Crane here comes very close to the Intentionalist School of Phenomenology, and in this respect he anticipates an important school of modern criticism.

Crane now goes on to suggest the procedure which will enable the critic to discover the intention of the author. He advises the critic to do two things, which constitute two distinctive parts of the procedure. What Crane says at this part of his essay elucidates his opinions on hypotheses. The critic at first, Crane suggests, tries to construct all the alternative hypotheses possible, beside one of his own preference, in a fashion that they are also of his own devising. He must try to collect supportable evidence for all of them even if it appears to him that his own hypothesis is more relevant and liable to fewer objections. The framing of a number of alternative hypotheses will enable the critic to judge the power and limitation of his own hypothesis. Here ends the first part of critical interpretation. However, the other part is even more important. Here the critic is required to take a different attitude to test the validity of his hypothesis. He should treat his own hypothesis in a manner that it has been proposed by someone else and try his best "to refute or qualify it by looking for relevant facts with which it is inconsistent wholly or in part" (Crane *Humanities* Vol. II 245). It will help the critic either to reject his hypothesis as a wrong one or to accept it as one containing the truth. This method is similar to what Sir Karl Popper in *The Poverty of Historicism* has called 'the method of selection by elimination.' The critic, he says, must frame all the possible hypotheses and then try to eliminate each one by showing its weakness. And in this process only that hypothesis which cannot be eliminated or rejected by any means may be accepted as fact.

Crane's observation on hypotheses or the way he suggests to establish a hypothesis as fact is obviously preferable to the traditional way of testing the truth of a hypothesis. The only objection that can be put against Crane's method is in relation to the objectivity of the critic. His method claims an objective mind which will be able to treat all the hypotheses, including one's own, equally in respect of importance. But in reality one may at least unconsciously, remain biased to one's own hypothesis. However, Crane's method is otherwise preferable. It will surely enable a single critic to perform the task of several critics through centuries. For, as we all know, one critic often points out the weaknesses of the critical observation of his predecessor and establishes his own observation in the same way of positive confirmation as his predecessor did. He again is often modified by a critic of his younger generation. What all these critics do is to expose the limitations of other's hypothesis and to collect supportable evidence in favour of his own. The approach of Crane can lead a single critic to try all the possible hypotheses and eliminate all but one. It may also keep a critic free from the undue influence or tyranny of a hypothesis.

Now in the light of his observation Crane examines Robertson's concept of historical criticism and the nature of hypothesis required to such a criticism. Robertson's idea is that the critic is required to form a workable conception of the intellectual background of a period as a whole, in the light of which he will be able to interpret all the works and ideas of that period. This idea leads Robertson and Huppe in their book on *Piers Plowman* to give such a conception of the Middle Ages. They suggest that the teaching of the church was at the centre of the intellectual and literary activities of the medieval period. Christianity or the Bible taught men to love their fellow men and to condemn self love. The interpretation of the Bible was not always in the literal level, but in the level of allegory. However, the interpretations of the Bible and the development in religious teaching of the period must have a great influence on the Christian poets of that time. Robertson calls it a workable concept of the intellectual background of the medieval age. His view is that this conception will serve for the critic as a principle of explanation applicable to all the poetic texts of the period and he claims that those texts of the period which have hitherto remained ambiguous and incoherent will appear meaningful and consistent when judged in the light of the intellectual background of the period.

Crane observes that what Robertson gives in the name of an workable concept of the intellectual background of the Middle Ages as a whole is not an "inventory of the many different 'intellectual' traditions at work in that period which the students of its literature ought to know about, but a formula assigning to one such tradition—the 'scriptural,' 'patristic,' 'exegetical' tradition—an architectonic status with respect to all particular intellectual and literary development of the age" (Crane *Humanities* Vol. 11 238). Crane also observes that this idea of the 'workable conception' of the medieval thought and its applicability to the poetic texts of that period can at best serve as a workable hypothesis. The critic, according to the theory of the privileged hypothesis, can think of the greater relevance of the allegorical tradition of the biblical exegesis to a full understanding of medieval poetry. But the claim of the Robertsonians is greater than that. They on the one hand give priority to the exegetical tradition over other possible sources of literary inspiration in the medieval period and, on the other, consider it relevant to explain all serious poetry written at that period. Crane's wise remark is that "they have thus transformed what is at most only a general working hypothesis—one capable of suggesting particular hypotheses about the possible meanings and devices of medieval poems, which then have to be tested independently—into a ruling hypothesis" (Crane *Humanities* Vol. II 255).

The Robertsonians like those scholars whom we generally call Freudians or Marxists give emphasis on some preferred principles of explanation, not on the set of problems to be solved. And the particular hypotheses framed by the critics of this group are those only which are in harmony with the critics' favourite explanatory principles. Their loyalty to their favourite explanatory principles prevent them from trying those hypotheses which are not in proper harmony with their principles. Crane also mentions Kant's distinction between 'determinant' and 'reflective' judgments in order to criticize the method of the Robertsonians. He observes, "What is fundamentally wrong with the Robertsonians and all other schools of interpretation that approach texts from the vantage point of a single preferred principle of explanation is their unconscious craving for 'determinant' judgments in a field where only 'reflective' judgments are possible by reason of the contingent and unpredictable nature of the subject matter" (Crane *Humanities* Vol. II 258).

Crane's judgment on Robertson is not attested by the history of critical response to Robertson's work. Robertson's monumental work entitled *Materials For the History of Thomas Backett, Archbishop of Canterbury,* edited for the Rolls Series by J.C. Robertson in seven volumes was published in 1875. The work is generally referred to as *Materials.* Even after one hundred years of its publication the book is regarded as a piece of sound scholarship and is referred to by scholars interested in the history of the period. T.S. Eliot also closely followed *Materials* while writing *Murder in the Cathedral.* So whatever may be the rationale of Robertson's hypothesis, the fact remains that the hypothesis is proved sound and valid.

III

"HISTORY VERSUS CRITICISM IN THE STUDY OF LITERATURE"

In the essay "History Versus Criticism in the Study of Literature" R.S. Crane has taken up a very practical problem faced by most universities today. In fact, this is a piece of what Eliot calls 'workshop criticism,' the craftsman talking about his craft. Here Crane discusses a problem that he has experienced as a teacher of literature and he wants to see things in the proper perspective and put them in order. The problem is basic to everybody concerned with literature. The problem is to determine the aim of teaching and studying the art of literature. The question involves directly those departments of colleges and universities which are concerned with this art. Crane himself was a professor of English and naturally he was aware of what actually goes on in the name of studying literary art. The essay actually acts as a form of self-criticism, the aim of which is to determine what ought to be the immediate purpose of the university departments involved in the teaching of literary art.

The immediate stimulus behind the essay however is two opposing statements given by two distinguished American professor-scholars in their attempts to answer the question of what should be the principal aim of studying literature. Howard Mumford Jones advocates in favour of historical study of literature. A literary scholar, in his opinion, should be the historian of literature, leaving the task of critical judgment to some others. But John Livingston Lowes, another professor of English, considers criticism to be the ultimate goal of literary study. His suggestion is that the end of all researches in the field of literature is criticism and he claims that one can, without any knowledge of the historical information understand and enjoy a work of literature, and can explain it in terms of his critical understanding.

The difference between Jones and Lowes however is not a difference simply of historical criticism and textual criticism. They do not actually speak about two different theories of criticism, but two different subjects namely 'literary history' and literary criticism. Crane realizes this point of difference as well as the importance of the issue. He feels that the functions of the university departments of literature will consequently change as they take up the one or the other as their principal aim. So he advances very cautiously and before passing his judgment on the issue, examines carefully the two programmes of literary studies—historical and critical—in order to realize the elements involved in them, and ascertain the nature of the knowledge they impart and the relevance of such knowledge to the study of literature. He also considers the practical situation of literary study under the present system to consider the results, good and bad, it yields.

Crane first considers the historical study of the art of literature and observes that the literary historian like the author of any other history tries to derive certain elementary propositions of facts as primary materials of his history. Biographies of authors, date of composition of a work, chief characteristics of the age in which a work is composed, clarifications of language and thought, sources of allusions and quotations used in a work, and such others may be considered as the rightful domain of a literary historian. But all these are only materials of the proposed history, not the history itself. They must be integrated into an explanatory narrative of the transformations undergone. In this respect it is worth recalling what Eliot observed: "Shakespeare acquired more essential history from Plutarch than most men could from the whole British museum" (Eliot *Sacred Wood* 52). The affinity between Eliot and Crane in their idea of history is worth noting. Both believe, by implication, that facts, events and documents do not constitute history; they are only materials of history. History is a pattern, a guiding force that arises out of the various interactions of these materials. History is essentially abstract, although it is an abstraction of concrete things. Sense of history, therefore, requires a vision, an intuitive apprehension of the reality of things beneath the debris of historical materials.

Crane defines literary history in this language: "A literary history, like any other history is a narrative of the changing habits, beliefs, attitudes, tastes, and purposes of individual persons and groups or organizations of persons living in particular times and places; it is not a history of literature but of literary men" (Crane *Humanities* Vol. II 7). From this definition the chief characteristics and limitations of such a history can thus, be arranged:

(a) It is more a history of authors and poets than of literature.

(b) The uncommon or accidental characteristics rather than the regular features are of primary interest.

(c) It (literary history) remains more or less indifferent to the literary or aesthetic value of an individual work. The textual sides remain neglected except in some general statements about the leading tendency of the works of the age in general.

(d) What follows from the point just mentioned is that the major and minor works are of equal importance to a literary historian, because his concern is not with the individual varieties, but with the leading tendencies of the age.

(e) A literary history is thus a storehouse of general information about literature, a record book of when, why and how certain changes in habit, belief, taste etc. took place. There is hardly any scope of interpreting and evaluating an individual work.

The value of writing and reading such a history, however, Crane rightly observes, is the same as writing and reading general history or history of other fine arts. It lies in "the satisfaction," Crane says, "of one's desire to know and to understand the significant transformations in human affairs" (Crane *Humanities* Vol. II 11). If we can accept this to be the ultimate aim of studying literature, we can welcome historical study of literature as our ideal. But very few of us, and quite reasonably, can be satisfied in accepting this to be the aim of literary study. Crane also considers it to be a very limited view. He, therefore, considers the other type of literary study, the aim of which is criticism.

By 'criticism' Crane here means only those analytical and *evaluative* statements about imaginative literature in which a literary work is considered as work of art primarily and not as a case-book of psychological study or a raw material for historical or sociological consideration. One may here accuse Crane of 'reductionism' because the view of criticism he holds in this essay is a restricted one. It is mainly textual criticism which he speaks of, keeping aside the extra-textual considerations. But we must not forget that Crane has here consciously used the word 'criticism' in this restricted sense with a special purpose in mind; and the purpose is to examine the purely aesthetic qualities of a literary work in order to see the elements involved in it and the result it ultimately yields. It is in sharp contrast with the historical study of literature. So the restriction of the meaning of the word 'criticism' is not an instance of reductionism. Crane is utterly against this tendency of the monistic critics as most of his writings show.

However, Crane examines the elements involved in criticism and the purpose they serve. Criticism is a reasoned discourse and to formulate this discourse some theories are required. But theories are not all; good theories cannot always be the guarantee for a successful criticism. Selection and application of the proper theory are equally important. So sensibility and feeling which enable a critic to select and apply the proper theory are also there in the background of an efficient criticism. But not merely these, there are certain texts which require some special knowledge of the language used and the allusions employed. These texts necessitate some sort of philosophical and stylistic research for their understanding, which is prior to any criticism. Understanding, however, can be at least of two types and it is in this point that a literary historian and a critic widely differ. The genetic or historical sense of understanding is the chief concern of the literary historian. It implies to ask and know 'why' an author has written something he has written. It is, in other words, to know the causes, mostly extra textual, behind the composition of a literary piece. The other sense in which the word 'understand' is used and which is the primary concern of the critic is the artistic sense of knowing 'what' it is that the author is saying as well as the technique of his saying so. Crane of course does not mean to say that the literary historian cannot have the second type of understanding or *vice versa*. Rather in the vein of his pluralistic attitude he allows the critic to take help of historical information if he thinks it necessary. But his point is that this type of historical understanding has hardly any direct relevance to the ends of critical interpretation or appraisal. Criticism is chiefly concerned with the structural, stylistic and aesthetic interpretations of texts with the help of certain theoretical principles and the critic's sensitive reactions to literary texts. And the peculiar value of criticism, Crane remarks, "would be measured by the extent to which it helped to conserve, in the midst of a university dominated by science and history, the proper interests of art" (Crane *Humanities* Vol. II 19).

In the concluding part of the essay Crane considers the practical situation of literary studies in different universities of today. Here he takes the role of an attentive observer of the systems of teaching and learning the art of literature. He finds that the professors and scholars of English in different universities devote their energies mostly to literary history rather than to criticism. In the class teaching programme, in setting up of papers and dissertations in different examinations, in selecting research topics and in almost everything it is the historical study that receives the preference. Questions related to biographical, bibliographical or other historical investigations are preferred, both by the teachers and the students, to the questions related to the artistic investigation of the texts. The result however is not inspiring. The young people who come out acquiring their highest university degrees often fail to understand and explain the textual properties of a literary work. They often fail to discuss a piece of poetry in terms of its artistic qualities and fail to justify what are peculiarly artistic in a work of art. They are rich only in historical information but aesthetically speaking they are almost barren. Few exceptions are of course there but credit must not go to the departments of English for creating the critical temperaments in those exceptional students. They are rather, in the phrase of Crane, 'self-taught.'

Thus Crane exposes the problem created by a remarkably great partiality to historical study of literature. And he suggests a thorough revision of the existing system reducing the time and importance devoted to literary history. But he does not exclude literary history from the scope of university teaching. He only suggests that the students must be informed of the fact that literary appreciation is there at the root of studying literature and that literary history has no direct contribution to such an artistic appreciation of literary texts. Crane in order to increase the ability of artistic appreciation suggests two distinct sorts of studies in all the levels starting from college. First, he suggests the study of certain theories about fine arts in general and the art of literature in particular. And the second part of literary education will be the application of the theories in the reading and literary explication of individual literary works.

Crane however warns that literary explications must not be allowed to "degenerate into linguistic or historical investigations or into mere occasions for the parading of personal tastes, but should be kept constantly directed toward their proper objective—the text itself considered as a production of art to be read appreciatively for its own sake in the light of relevant knowledge and of the principles of its kind" (Crane *Humanities* Vol. II 23). This emphasis on the 'explication of the text' is a New-Critical phenomenon. Like the New Critics Crane concentrates on the literary work itself. But he remains free from the critical myopia of the New Critics in his insistence on a theory and in his exploration of the relation between literary historiography and literary criticism. The text is primary. Various circumstances leading to the birth of a particular text are secondary. A knowledge of these circumstances would definitely increase our understanding and enjoyment of a text, but not its value. Value of the text depends entirely on the text itself. Thus Crane intends to improve the aesthetic sense of literary scholars and to keep proper balance between the two different sorts of literary studies mentioned by him at the opening of the essay.

The manner in which the whole subject is treated in the essay and given at the end a synthesized solution is quite typical of Crane. His pluralistic temperament always incites him to explain and realise all the theories and techniques to receive unhesitatingly the necessary parts of all which seem useful to attain his desired result. Here we find him analysing the apparently opposing ways of literary studies and to suggest the ideal way of studying literary works for the best outcome. He is never rash in his judgment. Only after considering all the possibilities he accepts liberally whatever becomes acceptable and rejects what is useless. This attitude is there at the root of Crane's pluralism.

Crane's originality, as the essay exemplifies, lies in setting things in a proper historical perspective without losing focus on the text in hand. He does not ban, unlike the New Critics, the extra-textual considerations from the scope of literary study, but rather hails them. The idea of complete and comprehensive literary study which Crane suggests in this essay consists of two different but related circles. The inner circle is confined to the text and the larger outer circle accommodates the context. The critic-scholar has to move from the text to the context. The context which includes the historical and other considerations helps and increases one's understanding and enjoyment of the text. Thus there remains no contradiction between critical and historical approaches to literature. One is complementary to the other.

IV

"VARIETIES OF DRAMATIC CRITICISM"

Crane in this essay concerns himself with the varieties of dramatic criticism available so far to seek out the conditions under which "the reading and study of dramatic criticism may help to advance rather than to hinder the realization" (Crane *Humanities* Vol. II 215) of the drama as an object to be witnessed on the stage and as an object to be read, contemplated and discussed. Crane at the very outset, makes it clear that his main interest is to examine the conditions which can enable the audience to enjoy a drama both as a literary art and as a performing art. His intention is to hit upon the fundamentals of the dramatic art with which dramatic criticism is intimately related. Critics generally formulate critical propositions about the dramatic art in general or about individual works of that art, and the students of drama try to utilize those propositions for their better understanding of the drama. The effects of studying such critical theories and propositions, however, are of two types. We are often moved so much by a persuasively argued doctrine about the drama that we attach ourselves to it almost dogmatically, paying only scant attention to other theories. The immediate consequence of such an attachment to a particular theory is that it restricts our power of observation. We can hardly look beyond those aspects of the drama, which our theory permits. Another possibility is that we may pick out the essential points from various critical theories and thus obtain an extensive knowledge of the dramatic art. It thus enables one to say more things about a play than a dogmatic follower of a particular theory can. But at the same time it must be admitted that one says too many things about the drama without knowing why one says them. What actually is the common defect of both these ways is that they lack a critical view about the criticism itself, and therefore accept the propositions as they are. In order to overcome this limitation and to really profit from various critical theories about the drama "we must form the habit of reading them with a view not merely to what they say about a given subject but to why they say this, whatever it may be, rather than something else" (Crane *Humanities* Vol. II 216). In other words, we should always try to find out the reasons or the compulsions which direct a dramatic critic to say what he says and not to say what other critics say. Crane's aim here is to examine this aspect of the dramatic criticism. Crane strikes at the very root of our aesthetic response and questions the rationale of it. Whatever one may feel it must emerge from a complex network of many other factors. It is this complex network that, on ultimate analysis, provides what Dryden called "grounds of criticism."

Crane observes that there are two fundamentally different ways of considering the drama. In one method the critic "holds that the truth about the drama must be deduced from the truth about something else, to which the drama is related as a part or a means" (Crane *Humanities* Vol. II 218). Plato was the early representative of this method and he initiated a long tradition of dramatic criticism in this way. The other method of dramatic criticism of which Aristotle was the early representative is that in which the critic discusses the drama "in terms of principles peculiar to the drama itself as a distinctive form of art" (Crane *Humanities* Vol. II 218). Crane has also observed that in spite of various additions, alterations and borrowings of elements from one another, these two modes of discussion have created two distinct traditions in the history of dramatic criticism.

A common characteristic of all the critical theories in the Platonic tradition of dramatic criticism is that the drama is essentially considered "as an activity or function in the context of other human activities or functions, and hence is governed by principles that signify or point to some larger good than that of the drama itself, a good which the drama ought to serve if it is to become what it can be or if it is to be tolerated in society" (Crane *Humanities* Vol. II 218). Plato in *The Republic* condemned drama in the light of the final good. By arousing passions and emotions of the audience drama may mislead the citizens of an ideal state. In *The Laws* where Plato has depicted the picture of the second-best state, he allows the drama under heavy censorship. The view of the drama expressed in *The Laws* and *The Republic*, however, is extremely negative. And this negative attitude, Crane observes, is reflected in the Puritan attack on the stage and also in the attempts of the moralists to prove the ethical imperfection and dangers of the stage.

Essentially the Platonic tradition of criticism is the tradition of moral criticism. Plato guided by his desire to establish the republic with ideal citizens, saw drama as a powerful moral instrument, because he was sure that drama through visual representation of the enactment of certain events could profoundly influence a man and control his course of action. When he rejected poetry, it may be regarded in this connection, it was because the poets were not conforming to the political ideas of *The Republic*. This moral tradition initiated by Plato continues through Sidney, Dr. Johnson, Bernard Shaw and is very much still there in the present critical climate. There is a consensus that theatre is useful in propagating certain views, and in influencing people through these propaganda.

However, Crane has rightly pointed out that the approaches of all the critics of this tradition are not equally negative. What a critic is required to do is to determine a set of ideas embodying some conception of the good of society and then to settle by mans of those ideas what the drama actually ought to be. Critics like Shaw, Eliot, Christopher Fry and Francis Fergueson have followed this method and have tried to show what the drama should actually be, what purposes it should try to fulfil. Shaw conceived that the stage must be a factory of thought, an elucidator of social conduct and also a prompter of conscience. His writings in the *Saturday Review* as a weekly critic are guided by such an idea of the stage. Eliot also believed that art gives us some perception of an order of life. And the dramatist also should strive to attain that ideal end of art. Eliot himself favoured poetic drama to attain such a goal. Thus the critics of this tradition are found to judge the drama on the basis of principles derived from their concept of larger human interest. They may differ in the ideals and aims they set up for the drama, but they are all guided by the concept that the drama must function in the context of other human activities.

The other tradition of dramatic criticism, initiated by Aristotle, stands in a sharp contrast with the Platonic tradition chiefly because "it is essentially a criticism of forms and techniques, and it seeks to establish criteria for these by considering not so much the social or moral function of drama as the necessities and possibilities determined for the dramatic artist by such things as the character of his medium, the nature of his subjects, the psychology of his audience, or the standards set by earlier practitioners of his art" (Crane *Humanities* Vol. II 221). There are two distinctive phases or we may say types of criticism in the Aristotelian tradition. The first phase consists in discussing the drama with particular emphasis on the various forms like tragedy and comedy. And in the other mode the general character of the drama irrespective of tragedies and comedies, the requirements and opportunities on the part of the playwrights are examined. Both the ways however were hinted at by Aristotle in the *Poetics.*

Aristotle's primary concern in the *Poetics,* however, was with the first one. He took tragedy and comedy as two forms of imitative poetry. For, in Aristotle's concept of poetry as imitation drama is also called poetry. A drama becomes a drama by virtue of the 'manner' (in the Aristotelian sense) of imitation. Thus, in Aristotle there is no conflict between drama and poetry—a conflict which arises in the later periods. Poetry for Aristotle is a character that "belongs to all imitations in words—and to these as wholes—by virtue simply of the fact that they are imitations" (Crane *Humanities* Vol. II 224). We should only bear in mind in the light of the available historical scholarship, that poetry for Aristotle simply meant what literature means for us. In other words poetry is the general term for any imaginative work. The word poetry as we all know comes from the Greek word 'poein' (to make). An artist is a maker or a creator (the word 'create' is derived from Latin 'cretare' which also means 'to make'). Poetry is the esemplastic imagination which involves in literary work. With this concept in mind Aristotle goes on to examine the tragedy and the comedy which are nothing but formal ends, and he then on the basis of the existing plays points out the essential nature of these various forms of the drama.

However, this concept of the dramatic forms as expounded by Aristotle stands in a sharp contrast with the concept of the later critics primarily because Aristotle's method of definition disappeared in them. Critics of the neoclassical era, many of them, were guided by the assumption that dramatic criticism is a question of determining what actions, characters, sentiments, moral and emotional effects are proper to the idea of comedy as distinct from tragedy or other forms. Whereas the critics of the 19th century under the influence of the idealist philosophy assumed that the discussion of dramatic forms "must start from something fundamental in the nature of human existence or thought that can be taken as the basic tragic or comic 'fact' or the basic tragic or comic view of life" (Crane *Humanities* Vol. II 228). A.W. Schlegel, Hegel and others were guided by this assumption in their attempts to determine the basis of tragedy. And in the recent years critics like Gilbert Murray, F.M. Cornford, Maud Bodkin etc. are trying to "renew our understanding of the existing forms of artistic drama by exploring the broad analogies between them and the more general forms of primitive religious ritual and myth, or of the unconscious operations of the psyche from which they must be supposed to have emerged" (Crane *Humanities* Vol. II 228-29). This is obviously the result of some important speculations in the field of analytical psychology and cultural anthropology. Crane here shows how the criticism of dramatic forms has gradually changed in different ways since Aristotle. But the fact remains that they are all criticism of dramatic forms.

The other variety of dramatic criticism in the Aristotelian tradition is that in which the critics do not concern themselves with the various dramatic forms but talk about the general principles required to constitute a play, whether it be a tragedy, a comedy or a farce. The possibility of such a criticism was only hinted in the *Poetics* but not elaborated. It takes its form in Castelvetro with his emphasis on the character of the theatrical audience as the first principle of dramatic criticism. And this criticism flourished mainly in the 19th and 20th centuries. The main problem of the critics practising this method is "how should plays, of whatever kind, be written if they are to be acceptable in theatres to the satisfaction of spectators?" (Crane *Humanities* Vol. II 230). A number of critics like schlegel, Gustav, Freytag, Francisque Sarcey and William Archer have tried to answer this in various ways. And the result is a body of advice to the playwrights about a great variety of things like dramatic technique, theme of a play, character, dialogue, choric devices, beginning and ending, scenes and a number of such others. Francisque Sarcey emphasized that the success of a play depends largely on the likings and dislikings of the audience. Hence, the satisfaction of the audience is the first principle of dramatic production. It is at this time, Crane shows, that the drama begins to be considered as a complete art form, totally separated from poetry. Naturally then the question of the relation between drama and poetry arises—the question which had no existence in Aristotle. And we must admit that the question has a great relevance today, when we can no longer identify drama with poetry. Poetry no longer means, as it meant for Aristotle, an imitation of human action; it rather suggests "a certain way of feeling or conceiving things, a certain power of unifying experience imaginatively" (Crane *Humanities* Vol. II 234). This renewed concepts of 'poetry' and 'drama' actually lead the critics on the one hand to claim the prestige of a complete art form for drama, and on the other to examine the drama from different standpoints. The changed situations form some sort of compulsive influence on the critics and direct them to theorize accordingly. Crane's point is that we must realize the situations as well as the influences on the critics first. Otherwise the critical propositions may seemingly contradict one another.

Crane thus gives us a brief account of the long history of evolutions and changes in the field of dramatic criticism. His credit lies as much in the act of exposing the various changes in the criticism of drama as in the act of categorizing the various conflicting views under three major traditions—one Platonic and the other two Aristotelian. He has successfully established his point that dramatic criticism in spite of all the differences among the theories of various critics, emerges essentially out of the three distinct traditions he has mentioned. His discussion helps us to pinpoint our attention on those three traditions. We are thus, saved from being puzzled by the great varieties of dramatic criticism. We can really enrich our understanding of a play by not attaching ourselves dogmatically to any one theory, but by realizing the relevance of each and every one.

V

"EVERY MAN HIS OWN CRITIC"

The right of critical evaluation of literary works has been practically monopolised nowadays by a group of learned scholars and writers of reviews in the papers. Most of the students or in a broader sense the majority of readers generally lack the power of critically judging literary works themselves, and depend upon the explanations and ideas of different theorists, teachers and literary critics for their understanding. They approach a literary work, whether it is to enjoy its aesthetic beauty or to evaluate it critically, with a set of previously known rules. In consequence their observations tend most of the times to be stereotyped, without any touch of individuality. Another common limitation is that they are often puzzled to explain a new piece of literary work if they do not get the help of explanatory notes. However, critical understanding is a thing, which is necessary for every individual reader for proper realisation of literary art. Everyone is thus required to be his own critic. Students of literature should be trained in such a way that they can master some sort of critical aptitude, think for themselves and arrive at independent judgments. But the type of education our students receive can hardly fulfil that purpose. Crane, therefore, suggests a different type of education, the aim of which will be to help the students to be better critics.

Crane exhibits the difference between the type of education students receive and the type they actually need to attain critical aptitude by means of an analogy of two professors of history. One of them, Professor A as Crane identifies him, took the task of teaching history as an act of "communicating effectively a concrete and self-contained subject matter; of putting before us a particular body of facts and generalisations which had presumably been thought about critically and independently by himself and others but which he didn't think about in our presence, and which it was our duty—our whole duty—merely to assimilate and remember as long as we could" (Crane *Humanities* Vol. II 196). The knowledge Professor A thus imparted to his students was mainly examination-oriented, which was sure to lose its initial poignancy when the examination was over because it was ready-made, leaving no scope for critical interaction. Professor B also admitted the importance of teaching particular historical subjects. But unlike professor A professor B did not accept this to be the ultimate aim of teaching history. He took as the end of his teaching the task of implanting in his students the discipline of history through the analytical and problematic mode of his lecturing. His aim was not to offer some brilliant interpretations of certain historical happenings but to make his students understand the basic principle of history—the "universally applicable way of considering human beings and their individual and collective actions, and of getting warranted knowledge concerning them" (Crane *Humanities* Vol. II 196). It helps the students to build within themselves a sense of history which is likely to remain with them even when they forget the particular incidents of history. The teaching of Prof. B inculcated what Eliot calls "universal intelligence." The students are made familiar with the fundamental historical principles through the illustrations of certain historical events. The students are thus better equipped to approach history than they are through the teachings of professor A. Crane, quite reasonably, prefers the teaching of professor B to that of professor A as a model to follow, and he suggests that this type of education is required to be given to the students of literature in order to make everyone of them his own critic.

The students, Crane suggests, should be taught certain elementary facts about literature in general. Side by side they should get sufficient exposure to various artistic problems which will refine their literary ideas and promote their discriminating judgment. These two should form the basic aims of teaching literary and critical arts. And with these in view the students should be given adequate training in different theoretical aspects as well as in practical criticism in order to develop within themselves the power of critical judgments.

A group of critics and reviewers, however, are always against the inclusion of literary theories in educational programmes. They hold the opinion that the students should not be burdened with a lot of abstract theories of literature; they should instead be trained to respond wholeheartedly to a literary work. Crane however opposes this view by saying that theories in one form or another are sure to come even when they are carefully kept aside. He maintains that those who reject theories in their pronouncements on education, make use of different theories in their essays, books and review articles. Crane shows strikingly original insights when he suggests that deliberate rejection of theories is also a theory. In other words, to say that no theory is needed is itself a theory. Surprisingly enough the students also somehow manage to absorb various theories in the course of their studies and make a conscious or unconscious use of them in their writings even when they are asked to write on the basis of their experience of certain literary works. So some theoretical concepts, whether well-understood or not, are inevitably there in the minds of the students. And the teachers' duty, Crane suggests, is to see that these concepts only promote not retard their proper understanding of literary works. For, critical theories may function both ways. They may stimulate a student's observations and judgments by drawing his attention to some aspects which, had he no acquaintance with the theories, he might easily overlook. It may be regarded to be the positive function of a theory. But a theory may negatively function in a student by restricting his observations and evaluations. He hardly approves any observation which his theory does not allow. This makes criticism narrow, constricted and badly parochial. This attitude runs counter to the humanistic, broad-based nature of literature. These almost opposing functions of critical theories are again due to how we possess them. Theories are taken either as "unexamined dogmas which we are under some compulsion to apply to whatever we read, or we may possess them as useful but necessarily limited hypotheses that may or may not be relevant to any particular case" (Crane *Humanities* Vol. II 202). The first one is actually the dogmatic stand, which always makes one's critical approach restricted, and the students, if they are not properly taught of this limited nature of literary theories, easily fall a victim to this stand.

Another point Crane here emphasises is that every critical doctrine depends for its meaning upon two things: (a) its philosophical foundation and (b) the common sense knowledge of literary principles. Crane refers to the difference between Aristotle and a group of moderns with regard to their concepts of plot to show that an analysis of the philosophical bases of critical doctrines may remove some apparent contradictions of various theoretical concepts. Common sense knowledge, that is the knowledge or ideas formed out of one's wide reading and practical understanding of literary texts, helps to build one's critical outlook. Mere common sense knowledge, however, is not sufficient for complete understanding of literary art. But the most important use of it is that the range of such knowledge is wider than the range of any critical theory and also that it helps us to test the validity of a critical theory by supplying equivalents for the problems related to various theories. It may thus act as a safeguard against theoretical misconceptions.

In the concluding part of the essay Crane speaks about practical criticism which, in his opinion, is equally important to develop critical abilities of the students. Practical criticism, which concentrates on the meanings, structures, artistic problems and values of individual literary works is an outcome of various 20th century critical movements, chiefly the New Criticism. Crane believes that the chief concern of a literary artist is not to express his philosophy of life, his cultural traditions and such others. All these find expression in a literary work only indirectly. The artist's chief concern is to solve certain artistic problems which he faces in the work in hand. And an important aim of practical criticism is to point out the problems and the ways in which the artist solves them. Crane also emphasises that a literary problem should be solved in terms of the author's immediate literary task. Thus, he justifies the fourth voyage of *Gulliver's Travels* from within the framework of the book, and "the little episode in chapters 6 and 8 of *Persuasion* which concerns the dead son of Anne Eliot's friend Mrs. Musgrove" (Crane *Humanities* Vol. II 211). Crane concentrates on that particular point in *Persuasion* where the episode occurs and shows how the episode was necessary in leading to the "emotional climax in the final reunion of the lovers." It was necessary to convince the reader that "Wentworth actually had other and better capabilities of feeling and action than his continuing resentment at Anne's earlier rejection of him allowed him to manifest in his dealings with her" (Crane *Humanities* Vol. II 213-14). It is really remarkable how Crane explores the "literary rationale of a literary work." The essay begins with a quotation from Eliot who is quoted again in the concluding section. This naturally suggests some affinity between Eliot and Crane in their attitude to literary criticism. Crane like Eliot believes that literary criticism should be literary and not something else. An adequate training of the students in this type of criticism, Crane believes, may build in them a habit of reading literary works in the light of some specific ends, problems and reasons. Their critical ability may thus be increased.

The most remarkable point in this essay is Crane's observation that successful understanding of literary art requires individual critical ability. So the necessity of giving proper training to the students to develop their critical aptitudes can hardly be doubted. The idea that Crane propounds in this essay is of enormous practical value and is perfectly in keeping with the basic position of the Chicago critics who start with the particular and then move out to the universal. This is one of the fundamental differences between New Critics and the Chicagoans. The New Critics concentrate on the particular and remain confined to the particular. The Chicagoans start with the particular but discover the universal principles in the particulars, and thus move out to the universal. In the teaching of history also the method should be inductive, moving from the particular events to the universal principles operating behind the particular incidents. Crane is interested in sharpening the critical faculty of the students and in developing their literary sensibility. This admittedly is a valuable objective of teaching literature and making every man his own critic. No approach can be perfect, and Crane's approach though extremely valuable and pragmatic, is also not free from certain lacuna arising out of the variable factors which concern the intellectual capacity of the students, their training and discipline. As there is a great variety of students in terms of calibre and intellect, aptitude and interest, there will be a great variety of critics even when all of them follow the method recommended by Crane. Even then it is expected that the difference among the students as critics will be only in degree, not in kind. This essay, to note one more point, has some affinity with another essay of Crane, namely "History *Versus* Criticism in the Study of Literature." There also Crane shows the importance of criticism or critical analysis of literary texts.

Works Cited in the Book

Aristotle, *On the Art of Poetry*, translated by Ingram Bywater, Delhi: Oxford University Press, 1985.

Clarke, Samuel, "The Great Duty of Universal Love," 1705.

Crane, R.S., *The Languages of Criticism and the Structure of Poetry*, Toronto: University of Toronto Press, 1953.

——, *The Idea of the Humanities and Other Essays Critical and Historical*, Vol. I, Chicago: The University of Chicago Press, 1967.

——, *The Idea of the Humanities and Other Essays Critical and Historical*, Vol. II, Chicago: The University of Chicago Press, 1967.

——, *Critical and Historical Principles of Literary History*, Chicago: The University of Chicago Press, 1971.

——, "Interpretation of Texts and the History of Ideas," *College English*, II, 1941.

——, (ed.), *Critics and Criticism, Ancient and Modern*, Chicago: The University of Chicago Press, 1952.

Eliot, T.S., *The Sacred Wood*, Delhi: B.I. Publications, 1982.

——, *Selected Essays*, London: Faber and Faber Ltd., 1963.

——, *On Poetry and Poets*, London: Faber and Faber Ltd., 1957.

——, "Poetry and Propaganda," *Bookman LXX*, 6, February, 1930.

Fekete, John, *The Critical Twilight*, London: Routledge and Kegan Paul Ltd., 1977.

Fletcher, F.T.H., *Montesquieu and English Politics 1750-1800*, London: Edward Arnold and Co., 1939.

Fowler, Roger (ed.), *A Dictionary of Critical Terms*, London: Routledge and Kegan Paul Ltd., 1987.

Frye, Northrop, *Anatomy of Criticism: Four Essays*, Princeton: Princeton University Press, 1957.

Glicksberg, C.I., *American Literary Criticism 1900-1950*, New York: Hendricks House Inc., 1951.

Hemingway, E., *The First Forty Nine Stories*, London: Jonathan Cape, 1939.

Jeffares, A. Norman, *Swift, Modern Judgments*, London: Macmillan, 1968.

Knights, L.C., Review of Crane's *The Language of Criticism and the Structure of Poetry, Review of English Studies*, Vol. VI, 1955.

Legouis, Emile and Louis Cazamian, *A History of English Literature*, London: J.M. Dent and Sons Ltd., 1961.

Levin, Harry, "Criticism in Crisis," *Contexts of Criticism*, Cambridge, 1957.

Litz, A. Walton, "Literary Criticism," *Harvard Guide to Contemporary American Writing*, Daniel Hoffman (ed.), Delhi: Oxford University Press, 1959.

Locke, John, *Essay Concerning Human Understanding*, Book II.

Lodge, David (ed.), *20th Century Criticism*, London: Longman Group Ltd., 1972.

Lovejoy, A.O., *Essays in the History of Ideas*, Baltimore: The Johns Hopkins Press, 1948.

Mencken, H.L., *Prejudices, First Series*, New York: 1919.

Olson, Elder (ed.), *Aristotle's 'Poetics' and English Literature: a Collection of Critical Essays*, Chicago: The University of Chicago Press, 1965.

Olson, Elder, "An Outline of Poetic Theory," *Critics and Criticism*, R.S. Crane (ed.), Chicago: The University of Chicago Press, 1957.

Phillips, William, "New Criticism to Structuralism," *Partisan Review*, Vol. 47, 1980.

Pottle, F.A., *The Idiom of Poetry*, Ithaca, 1946.

Pritchard, J.P., *Criticism in America*, Ludhiana: Lyall Book Depot, 1970.

Ransom, J.C., "The Intent of the Critic," *Criticism as Pure Speculation*, Donald A. Stauffer (ed.),: Princeton, 1941.

Ransom, J.C., *The New Criticism*, Norfolk Conn: New Directions, 1941.

Ray, M.K., "Objectivity in Literary Criticism," *Criticism and Research*, Vol. 8, 1987-88.

Ray, M.K., *Change in Language and Literature*, Proceedings of the 16th Triennial Congress of the International Federation of Modern Languages and Literatures, held in Budapest, Hungary, Aug. 22-27, 1984, ed. by Hiklos Szabelesi and Jozsef Kovaes, Budapest: Akademiai Kiado, 1986.

Richards, I.A., *Principles of Literary Criticism*, London: Routledge and Kegan Paul Ltd., 1963.

Sampson, George, *The Concise Cambridge History of English Literature*, Cambridge: Cambridge University Press, 1965.

Sidney, Sir Philip, *An Apologie for Poetrie*, Cambridge: Cambridge University Press, 1951.

Spingarn, J.E., *Creative Criticism and Other Essays*, New York, 1952.

Tate, Allen, *On the Limits of Poetry: Selected Essays 1928-48*, New York, 1941.

Trilling, Lionel, *The Liberal Imagination*, New York: The Viking Press Inc., 1950.

Vivas, Eliseo, "The New Aristotelians of Chicago," *Swanee Review*, Spring, 1943.

Watson, George, *The Literary Critics*, London: Penguin, 1964.

Wellek, René, *A History of Modern Criticism 1750-1950*, New Haven: Yale University Press, 1986.

Williams, K.M., "Gulliver's Voyage to the Houyhnhnms," *Swift, Modern Judgments*, A.N. Jeffares (ed.), London: Macmillan.

Winters, Yvor, *In Defence of Reason*, Denver: Swallow, 1947.

——, *The Function of Criticism: Problems and Exercises*, London: Routledge and Kegan Paul, 1962.

Select Bibliography

Major Works of R.S. Crane

Crane, R.S., *The Languages of Criticism and the Structure of Poetry*, Toronto: University of Toronto Press, 1953.

——, *The Idea of the Humanities and Other Essays, Critical and Historical*, Vol. I, Chicago: The University of Chicago Press, 1967.

——, *The Idea of the Humanities and Other Essays, Critical and Historical*, Vol. II, Chicago: The University of Chicago Press, 1967.

——, *Critical and Historical Principles of Literary History*, Chicago: The University of Chicago Press, 1971.

——, "Review of Paul F. Saintonge *et. al.*, Horace: Three Phases of His Influence," *Philological Quarterly*, Vol. XVI, April, 1937.

——, "Interpretation of Texts and the History of Ideas," *College English, II*, 1941.

——, "Two Essays in Practical Criticism," *University Review*, Vol. VIII, 1942.

——, "Semantics and the Teaching of Prose Literature," *College English, IV*, 1942.

——, "English Neoclassical Criticism: An Outline Sketch," *Dictionary of World Literature*, Joseph T. Shipley (ed.), 1943.

——, "I.A. Richards and the Art of Interpretation," *Ethics, LIX*, 1947.

——, "Cleanth Brooks: Or, The Bankruptcy of Critical Monism," *Modern Philosophy*, Vol. XLV, 1948.

——, "The Rationale of the Fourth Voyage," *Gulliver's Travels: An Annotated Text with Critical Essays*, Robert A. Greenberg (ed.), New York, 1961.

——, (ed.), *Critics and Criticism, Ancient and Modern,* Chicago: The University of Chicago Press, 1952.

Secondary Materials

Abrams, M.H., *The Mirror and the Lamp: Romantic Theory and the Critical Tradition,* New York: Oxford University Press, 1953.

Aristotle, *On the Art of Poetry,* translated by Ingram Bywater, Delhi: Oxford University Press, 1985.

Barker, Ernest A., *The History of the English Novel,* Vol. VI, New York: Barnes and Noble, Inc., 1929.

Bodkin, Maud, *Archetypal Patterns in Poetry: Psychological Studies of Imagination,* New York: Vintage Books, 1958.

Booth, Wayne C., *Rhetoric of Fiction,* Chicago: the University of Chicago Press, 1961.

Bradbury, John M., *The Fugitives: A Critical Account,* New York: University of North Carolina Press, 1958.

Brooks, Cleanth, *The Well Wrought Urn: Studies in the Structure of Poetry,* New York: Harcourt, Brace and Company, 1947.

Brooks, C. and Warren, R.P., *Understanding Poetry,* New York: Holt, Rinehart and Winston, 1960.

Cargil, O., *Towards A Pluralistic Criticism,* Southern Illinois University Press, 1965.

Coleridge, S.T., *Biographia Literaria,* ed. J. Shawcrows, London: Rest Fenner, 23, Paternoster Row, 1958.

Collingwood, R.G., *The Idea of History,* Oxford: Oxford University Press, 1976.

Daiches, David, *Critical Approaches to Literature,* Bombay: Orient Longman, 1956.

Eagleton, Terry, *Literary Theory, An Introduction,* New Delhi: Doaba Publications, 2000.

Eliot, T.S., *The Sacred Wood,* Delhi: B.I. Publications, 1982.

——, *Selected Essays,* London: Faber and Faber Ltd., 1963.

——, *On Poetry and Poets,* London: Faber and Faber Ltd., 1957.

Empson, William, *Seven Types of Ambiguity,* London: Chatto and Windus, 1930.

Fekete, John, *The Critical Twilight*, London: Routledge and Kegan Paul Ltd., 1977.

Fletcher, F.T.H., *Montesquieu and English Politics 1750-1800*, London: Edward Arnold and Co., 1939.

Frye, Northrop, *Anatomy of Criticism: Four Essays*, Princeton: Princeton University Press, 1957.

Gardner, Helen, *The Business of Criticism*, London: Oxford University Press, 1959.

George, A.G., *Critics and Criticism*, Bombay: Asia Publishing House, 1962.

Glicksberg, C.I., *American Literary Criticism 1900-1950*, New York: Hendricks House Inc., 1951.

Grebstein, S.N., *Perspective in Contemporary Criticism: A Collection of Recent Essays by American English and European Literary Critics*, New York: Harper and Row Publishers, 1966.

Handy, W.J. and Max Wastbrook, *Twentieth Century Criticism: The Major Statements*, 1974, Indian rpt., New Delhi: Light and Life Publishers, 1976.

Harry Blamires, *A History of Literary Criticism*, Delhi: Macmillan India Ltd., 1991.

Hoffman, Daniel (ed.), *Harvard Guide to Contemporary American Writing*, Delhi: Oxford University Press, 1981.

Holloway, John, *The Charted Mirror*, London: Routledge and Kegan Paul Ltd., 1961.

Hyman, S.E., *The Armed Vision*, New York: Alfred A. Knoff, 1948.

Jeffares, A. Norman, *Swift, Modern Judgments*, London: Macmillan, 1968.

Jeffares, Ann and David Robey (ed.), *Modern Literary Theory: A Comparative Introduction*, London: B.T. Batsford Ltd., 1986.

Kaur, Tejinder, *R.S. Crane: A Study in Critical Theory*, New Delhi: Atlantic Publishers and Distributors, 1990.

Law Edmund, *Considerations on the state of the World with Regard to the Theory of Religion*, Cambridge, 1745.

Legouis, Emile and Louis Cazamian, *A History of English Literature*, London: J.M. Dent and Sons Ltd., 1961.

Lodge, David (ed.), *20th Century Criticism*, London: Longman Group Ltd., 1972.

——, (ed.), *Modern Criticism and Theory, A Reader*, London and New York: Longman, 1991.

Lovejoy, A.O., *Essays in the History of Ideas*, Baltimore: The Johns Hopkins Press, 1948.

——, *The Great Chain of Being*, New York: Harper Torchbooks, 1960.

Man, Paul de, *Blindness and Insight: Essays in the Rhetoric of Contemporary Criticism*, New York: Oxford University Press, 1971.

Nichols, S.G. (ed.), *Concept of Criticism*, New Haven: Yale University Press, 1963.

Olson, Elder (ed.), *Aristotle's 'Poetics' and English Literature: a Collection of Critical Essays*, Chicago: The University of Chicago Press, 1965.

Pottle, F.A., The *Idiom of Poetry*, Ithaca, 1946.

Pritchard, J.P., *Criticism in America*, Ludhiana: Lyall Book Depot, 1970.

Prasad, B., *An Introduction to Literary Criticism*, Oxford: Pergamon Press, 1965.

Raj Nath, *Essays in Criticism*, Delhi: Doaba House, 1971.

Ransom, J.C., *The New Criticism*, Norfolk Conn: New Directions, 1941.

Ray, Mohit K., *Studies in Literary Criticism*, New Delhi: Atlantic Publishers and Distributors, 2001.

——, (ed.) *Perspectives On Criticism*, New Delhi: Atlantic Publishers and Distributors, 2002.

Richards, I.A., *Principles of Literary Criticism*, London: Routledge and Kegan Paul Ltd., 1963.

Roberts, Mark, *The Fundamentals of Literary Criticism*, Oxford: Basic Blackwell, 1974.

Sampson, George, *The Concise Cambridge History of English Literature*, Cambridge: Cambridge University Press, 1965.

Schreider, S.M., *An Introduction to Literary Criticism*, Oxford: Pergamon Press, 1965.

Scott, W.S., *Five Approaches of Literary Criticism: An Arrangement of Contemporary Critical Essays*, New York: N.Y. Collier Books, 1962.

Sidney, Sir Philip, *An Apologie for Poetrie*, Cambridge University Press, 1951.

Simonson, H.P., *Strategies in Criticism*, New York: Holt, Rinchard and Winston, Inc., 1971.

Spiller, R.E., *A Time of Harvest: American Literature 1910-1960*, New York: Hill and Wang, 1962.

Spingarn, J.E., *Creative Criticism and Other Essays*, New York, 1952.

Stallman, R.W. (ed.), *Critiques and Essays in Criticism*, Routledge and Kegan Paul Ltd., 1960.

Stauffer, D.A. (ed.), *Criticism as Pure Speculation*, Princeton, 1941.

Stovall, F. (ed.), *The Development of American Literary Criticism*, University of North Carolina Press, 1955.

Sutton, Walter and Richard Foster. (ed.), *Modern Criticism: Theory and Practice*, New York: Odyssey Press, 1963.

Tate, Allen, *On the Limits of Poetry: Selected Essays 1928-48*, New York, 1941.

Trilling, Lionel, *The Liberal Imagination*, New York: The Viking Press Inc., 1950.

——, *The Last Decade: Essays and Reviews 1965-75*, Diana Trilling (ed.), Oxford: OUP, 1982.

Watson, George, *The Literary Critics*, London: Penguin, 1964, Vol. 6.

Wellek, René, *A History of Modern Criticism 1750-1950*, New Haven: Yale University Press, 1986.

——, and Austin Warren, *Theory of Literature*, Penguin, 1949.

Winters, Yvor, *In Defence of Reason*, Denver: Swallow, 1947.

——, *The Function of Criticism: Problems and Exercises*, London: Routledge and Kegan Paul, 1962.

INDEX

T

U

V

W